TRAILS WEST

PEOPLE
WHO MADE
HISTORY

SUSAN B. ANTHONY

Brenda Stalcup, *Book Editor*

Daniel Leone, *President*
Bonnie Szumski, *Publisher*
Scott Barbour, *Managing Editor*

Greenhaven Press, Inc., San Diego, CA

Every effort has been made to trace the owners of copy-righted material. The articles in this volume may have been edited for content, length, and/or reading level. The titles have been changed to enhance the editorial purpose. Those interested in locating the original source will find the complete citation on the first page of each article.

Library of Congress Cataloging-in-Publication Data

Susan B. Anthony / Brenda Stalcup, book editor.
    p. cm. — (People who made history)
    Includes bibliographical references and index.
    ISBN 0-7377-0890-5 (pbk. : alk. paper) —
ISBN 0-7377-0891-3 (lib. : alk. paper)
    1. Anthony, Susan B. (Susan Brownell), 1820–1906.
2. Feminists—United States—Biography. 3. Suffragists—United States—Biography. 4. Women social reformers—United States—Biography. 5. Women's rights—United States—History. I. Stalcup, Brenda. II. Series.

HQ1413.A55 S87   2002
305.42'092—dc21   2001051233
[B]

Cover photo: Library of Congress
Library of Congress, 36, 49, 78, 100, 107, 159

Copyright © 2002 by Greenhaven Press, Inc.
10911 Technology Place
San Diego, CA 92127
Printed in the U.S.A.

CONTENTS

Chapter 1: Anthony's Early Years: The Making of an Activist

Chapter 2: The Leader of the Women's Rights Movement

played a crucial role in the drive to open the university in her hometown to female students.

Anthony developed into an effective orator during years of working the lecture circuit, promoting the cause of women's rights throughout the United States.

Chapter 3: Anthony's Relationships with Her Colleagues

Once close friends and coworkers, Susan B. Anthony and Lucy Stone increasingly found themselves at odds over both personal issues and their goals for the suffrage movement. Their conflict was a contributing factor to the division of the movement in 1869.

Belying her reputation as a man-hater, Anthony actually welcomed the support of male allies who were sympathetic to the cause of women's suffrage.

The aging Anthony made a special effort to discover talented newcomers to groom as her successors in the women's rights movement and to carry on her battle for women's suffrage.

Beginning in Anthony's final years, the younger generation of feminists idolized her; after her death, they transformed her into an immortal symbol of the suffrage movement.

FOREWORD

In the vast and colorful pageant of human history, a handful of individuals stand out. They are the men and women who have come variously to be called "great," "leading," "brilliant," "pivotal," or "infamous" because they and their deeds forever changed their own society or the world as a whole. Some were political or military leaders—kings, queens, presidents, generals, and the like—whose policies, conquests, or innovations reshaped the maps and futures of countries and entire continents. Among those falling into this category were the formidable Roman statesman/general Julius Caesar, who extended Rome's power into Gaul (what is now France); Caesar's lover and ally, the notorious Egyptian queen Cleopatra, who challenged the strongest male rulers of her day; and England's stalwart Queen Elizabeth I, whose defeat of the mighty Spanish Armada saved England from subjugation.

Some of history's other movers and shakers were scientists or other thinkers whose ideas and discoveries altered the way people conduct their everyday lives or view themselves and their place in nature. The electric light and other remarkable inventions of Thomas Edison, for example, revolutionized almost every aspect of home-life and the workplace; and the theories of naturalist Charles Darwin lit the way for biologists and other scientists in their ongoing efforts to understand the origins of living things, including human beings.

Still other people who made history were religious leaders and social reformers. The struggles of the Arabic prophet Muhammad more than a thousand years ago led to the establishment of one of the world's great religions—Islam; and the efforts and personal sacrifices of an American reverend named Martin Luther King Jr. brought about major improvements in race relations and the justice system in the United States.

Each anthology in the People Who Made History series begins with an introductory essay that provides a general overview of the individual's life, times, and contributions. The group of essays that follow are chosen for their accessibility to a young adult audience and carefully edited in consideration of the reading and comprehension levels of that audience. Some of the essays are by noted historians, professors, and other experts. Others are excerpts from contemporary writings by or about the pivotal individual in question. To aid the reader in choosing the material of immediate interest or need, an annotated table of contents summarizes the article's main themes and insights.

Each volume also contains extensive research tools, including a collection of excerpts from primary source documents pertaining to the individual under discussion. The volumes are rounded out with an extensive bibliography and a comprehensive index.

Plutarch, the renowned first-century Greek biographer and moralist, crystallized the idea behind Greenhaven's People Who Made History when he said, "To be ignorant of the lives of the most celebrated men of past ages is to continue in a state of childhood all our days." Indeed, since it is people who make history, every modern nation, organization, institution, invention, artifact, and idea is the result of the diligent efforts of one or more individuals, living or dead; and it is therefore impossible to understand how the world we live in came to be without examining the contributions of these individuals.

Introduction: Susan B. Anthony's Campaign for Women's Rights

Born on February 15, 1820, in the quiet farming town of Adams, Massachusetts, Susan Brownell Anthony was the second child of Lucy Read and Daniel Anthony. Her parents eventually had eight children in all, six of whom—four girls and two boys—survived to adulthood. In many respects, Anthony's early childhood was unremarkable: She was raised in a stable home overseen by two devoted parents and surrounded by a close-knit extended family. She showed no signs of being a tomboy, nor overly sensitive to society's injustices, nor a natural leader. There were few hints that this little girl would grow up to change her world.

The Two Spheres

The world into which Susan B. Anthony was born placed numerous strictures on women, the legacy of centuries of tradition and law. Men and women were thought of as occupying separate spheres, sharply divided between public and private life. The public realm was considered men's domain. Most of their time and energy was spent outside the home: working, participating in local community events, engaging in politics, debating the controversies of the day. Women, on the other hand, were expected to devote themselves to the domestic sphere, centering their activities around the home and paying little attention to outside affairs.

Whether married or single, all women were affected by this tradition of the separate spheres. Women were not allowed to vote, to serve on juries, or to hold elective office. In fact, they were not even supposed to have their own political opinions, much less voice them. St. Paul's biblical assertion that women should keep silent in church was taken literally throughout most of the United States and was applied in nonreligious public settings. A proper woman would never dare to address a "mixed" audience of men and women, no matter how strong her feelings on the issue at hand. Education for girls was sparse, and most institutions of higher education—including all colleges and universities—refused to admit women.

The status of married women was even more restricted by the concept of coverture, which held that a wife's legal identity was subsumed by her husband's. This legal practice was greatly influenced by English jurist William Blackstone's *Commentaries on the Laws of England*, which stated:

> By marriage the husband and wife are one person in law; that is, the very being or legal existence of the woman is suspended during the marriage, or at least incorporated and consolidated into that of the husband; under whose wing, protection and cover, she performs everything.

Theoretically, coverture served to protect women by placing their public affairs in the capable hands of their husbands, who were familiar with the outside world and would look out for their wives' best interests. In reality, under coverture, married women lost many of the rights that they possessed while single. Once wed, a woman could no longer buy or sell property, sign contracts, or make a will without her husband's approval. Any land or other personal property that a woman brought with her into a marriage, or that she inherited later, fell under her husband's control; if he decided to sell her property against her wishes, she had no legal recourse to stop him. Similarly, any money she earned through the work of her own hands belonged legally to her husband.

The limitations to married women's rights extended beyond financial matters. For a woman to obtain a divorce was very difficult—even in cases of extreme cruelty or abandonment—and custody of the children was almost invariably granted to the husband. (Even widows had no automatic right to the custody of their children; it was not uncommon for a husband's will to specify that his children be placed in the care of his relatives, who could, if they so desired, legally deny contact with the children from their mother.) Another result of coverture was that married women literally did not have the right to their own bodies. In a time when women faced a high risk of death in childbirth and when reliable birth control methods were rarely attainable, wives often tried to avoid pregnancy by limiting their sexual availability.

However, as historians Lana Rakow and Cheris Kramarae point out, "sexuality in marriage [was considered] a woman's duty" rather than her "free choice"; if her husband objected, a woman usually had no real option but to obey his wishes. Likewise, in most regions of the United States, men still had the legal right to punish their wives by the use of physical force.

Single women were not bound by coverture, and in theory they had more rights over their private property and wages. In actuality, though, single women typically found themselves in a tenuous position, both legally and socially. Most single women did not live alone, a situation that would have been considered socially unacceptable. Instead, a single woman resided either with her parents or in the household of a married sibling or other family member. There she was expected to contribute to the functioning of the domestic sphere, helping with household chores and childcare. Her legal affairs—including control of her property or inheritances—were usually handled by a male relative without her input. If a single woman worked outside the home, she often was required to turn over her wages to the male head of the household where she lived.

For both single and married women, the available jobs were exceedingly narrow. Single women had a little more in the way of choice, since some careers such as teaching were off-limits to married women. Regardless of marital status, however, women could only find respectable employment in a few fields. The primary occupations open to them—teacher, governess, nanny, maid, seamstress, laundress—were considered part of the domestic sphere, involving some aspect of childcare or housework. At the time of Anthony's birth, it was also becoming acceptable for women to work in factories, especially textile mills engaged in the production of cloth. But whether working in a factory or teaching in a school, whenever women were employed in a job also open to men, they invariably made less money—sometimes less than one-fourth of the wages paid to men doing the same work.

Into this world Susan B. Anthony was born, but she would not leave it as she had found it. In every area mentioned above—in every respect that women's lives were limited—Anthony worked to remedy the injustices she found, to expand women's rights, to widen women's sphere to encompass the public world as well as the private.

A QUAKER CHILDHOOD

Although Anthony's childhood was rather ordinary, one aspect seems especially likely to have influenced her future career; that is, her upbringing as a Quaker. The Society of Friends (commonly known as Quakers) was unique among religious groups of this era in its advanced treatment of women. Men and women were innately equal in the eyes of God, the Quakers maintained. In their religious services, called meetings, women were allowed to speak as the spirit moved them. Quaker women also took equal part in church affairs and openly expressed their opinions about matters of church business and governance. Even more unusual for the time, Quaker women could serve as clergy. Anthony's grandmother and great-grandmother both attained the position of elder, the highest seat in the church; her aunt, a well-known minister, was frequently asked to preach at the annual Quaker meetings of New York state. "Because of her Quaker upbringing," historian Judith E. Harper explains, "Anthony grew up never questioning her right to voice her opinions or her equal opportunity to assume an active public role in society."

Quakers were also set apart from their neighbors by their commitment to plainness, by which they meant a simplicity in dress and mannerisms. They wore drab clothes without ruffles or jewelry, referred to each other as "thee" and "thou," and did not drink, dance, listen to music, or play cards and games. They were pacifists, refusing to fight in wars or serve in the army; some Quakers even refused to vote or pay taxes in protest against the government's military involvement. Liberal Quakers, including Anthony's family, placed great emphasis on progressive social causes, such as abolitionism and temperance. Anthony was raised in a religious environment that stressed the importance of the individual, standing up for one's principles, and working for the common good.

The egalitarian views of the Quakers often carried over into their family life, and Daniel Anthony was a case in point. Unlike many fathers of this era, he never favored his sons above his daughters. Indeed, he took great pains to ensure that Susan and her sisters received a thorough education and experience working outside the home. When the local school proved inadequate, Daniel started a private school at home for his children, staffed with the most highly educated teachers he could find. He made sure that his daughters learned math as well as embroidery, science as well as knitting. In addition, he developed an employment plan for his daughters: At the age of fifteen, each girl would begin teaching in the Anthonys' home school. As they gained experience, they would move on to jobs as governesses in private homes and teachers in the public schools. Susan and her sisters did not need to work; Daniel Anthony was a prosperous businessman who could easily afford to support his daughters at home, as was customary among members of the middle class. His decision was criticized by his neighbors, Harper writes, "who believed that it was improper for a man of his social standing to allow his daughters to work." Never a conformist, Daniel ignored their remarks; he felt it was essential for all his children, whether male or female, to learn to be self-supporting and independent.

Daniel also believed in the importance of higher education for his daughters. In 1836, he enrolled his oldest daughter, Guelma, in a Quaker boarding school for young women; Susan joined her there the following year. Susan's experiences at the boarding school were mixed. On one hand, she valued the opportunity to further her education and enjoyed the camaraderie she shared with her fellow students. On the other hand, she developed a severe case of homesickness, made worse by the fact that nothing she did seemed to be good enough for the demanding headmistress, Deborah Moulson. A pious and strict Quaker, Moulson endeavored to instruct her charges in morals as well as academics. She was also dying of tuberculosis, and the strain of her deteriorating health may have caused her to be more stern with her students than normal. Moulson singled out Susan for constant criticism, in sharp contrast to Guelma, who appeared to her envious sister to be the teacher's pet. When Susan confronted her teacher about this discrepancy, Moulson replied, "Thy sister Guelma does the best she is capable of, but thou dost not. Thou hast greater abilities and I demand of thee the best of thy capacity." Susan never felt able to measure up to Moulson's high expectations, but the experience left her with a lifelong tendency for relentless self-scrutiny and self-improvement.

MAKING HER OWN WAY

Susan's education was cut short by the failure of her father's businesses in the economic depression known as the panic of 1837. In May 1838, Guelma and Susan returned home from the boarding school to discover that their family was close to bankruptcy. Within the year, their father lost his factory and mills, his general store, and the family home. Susan took a teaching position, this time to help support her family. In the spring of 1839, when the Anthonys' house and its contents were auctioned off to pay their creditors, Susan was able to use her savings from her job to buy back some of her parents' personal belongings. Over the next few years, she embarked on a career in education, working sometimes as a governess, sometimes as a teacher in both public and boarding schools. Her parents rented an old tavern in Hardscrabble, New York, taking in boarders and travelers to make ends meet. Whenever Susan's job was close enough, she lived with her parents and helped out with the chores around the inn. Life was hard, but the monotony of work was relieved by a new surge in socializing: More than ever before, Susan's family received invitations to quilting parties, picnics, and other entertainments. Their house seemed to always be filled with sympathetic friends, relatives, and neighbors. In fact, Susan's mother later referred to the period after the bankruptcy as the happiest time of her life.

Part of this flurry of activity was undoubtedly due to the fact that the three eldest Anthony daughters were now of marriageable age. Along with her sisters, Susan joined in the social life of the town's young people, attending parties, going on buggy rides, and accepting visits from gentlemen callers. The diary she kept at the time is full of references to various young men, comparing their looks and their personalities, singling out some for special praise. But in an era when many women so dreaded the possibility of becoming a spinster that they would marry the first man who asked them, Susan B. Anthony was uncommonly strong-minded. During her twenties, she turned down a number of marriage proposals, and she continued to fend off unwelcome suitors well into her fifties.

In 1845, Anthony's parents moved again, this time to a farm in Rochester, New York. Here their financial outlook improved greatly. When Anthony accepted a position the following year as the headmistress of female students at the prestigious Canajoharie Academy, her salary no longer had to be earmarked for the support of her family. She also received her first exposure to life in a non-Quaker home when she moved in with her married cousin, Margaret Caldwell. Under these influences, Anthony began to abandon some of her Quaker ways. She went on a buying spree, indulging herself in colorful dresses, stylish capes, and decorative hats. She accepted invitations to dances, concerts, and the theater. But she retained her adamant disapproval of drinking liquor, eventually joining the local chapter of the Daughters of Temperance.

Anthony stayed in Canajoharie for three years, garnering praise from the community as an intelligent, proficient, and well-qualified schoolmistress. She was growing tired of teaching, however, and felt increasingly restless. To her dismay, she realized that she had reached the pinnacle of her profession, with little chance for further promotion and none whatsoever for receiving the same pay as her male counterparts. In the spring of 1849, she tendered her resignation to the academy with the intent of returning to the family farm at Rochester, but she decided to stay in Canajoharie long enough to see her cousin through a difficult pregnancy.

Margaret Caldwell did not recover her health after the baby was born, and Anthony nursed her through several weeks of dismal suffering. She was appalled at the lack of sympathy shown by Joseph Caldwell, Margaret's husband. On one occasion, for example, Joseph complained of a headache; when Margaret gently reminded him that she had had one for weeks, he replied, "Mine is the real head ache, genuine pain, yours is a sort of natural consequence [of childbirth]." Anthony shouldered all the responsibilities of the sickroom and childcare, but Joseph coldly rejected the suggestion that the new baby be named after Susan.

Despite Anthony's devoted care, Margaret Caldwell died. Heartsick and weary, Anthony headed home to Rochester. She was twenty-nine years old, disillusioned with the idea of marriage, bored with her chosen career—in every way, at loose ends.

THE BIRTH OF A REFORMER

Anthony's parents welcomed her home with open arms; if she needed a respite from teaching, they were more than happy to give her some time to reevaluate her goals and decide on a new course. Daniel was now selling insurance and had his hands full developing a clientele, so he offered his daughter the opportunity to run the family farm.

Anthony also joined the local temperance society and was soon busily involved in its activities. More and more, she longed to devote herself to a worthy cause, and temperance seemed a logical choice. Her family had always been firmly opposed to alcohol, considering it the source of much poverty and domestic violence. Additionally, as Professor Kathleen Barry points out, "temperance reform provided one of the few legitimate public outlets for women's moral concerns at this time." Anthony could plan fundraisers, travel to neighboring towns to organize new chapters, and attend temperance conventions without raising any eyebrows.

Meanwhile, the Anthonys' farm was quickly becoming a hotbed of abolitionism. A group of anti-slavery Quakers began meeting there on Sunday afternoons, often joined by prominent activists such as Frederick Douglass, William Lloyd Garrison, and Wendell Phillips. Anthony listened avidly to their discussions of the evils of slavery and their work to bring about the emancipation of the slaves.

And there was yet another reform movement springing up in the small towns of western New York. In July 1848, while Anthony was still in Canajoharie, the first-ever convention on women's rights took place in the village of Seneca Falls. The force behind the Seneca Falls convention was Elizabeth Cady Stanton, a local wife and mother involved in the anti-slavery movement. While studying the problem of slavery, Stanton began to see parallels between the legal status of slaves and women, especially married women who were bound by the restrictions of coverture. Along with some friends, Stanton organized the Seneca Falls convention as a forum for discussion of these issues. She also drew up a list of resolutions calling for equal rights for women, including the right to vote.

Anthony found the newspaper accounts of the Seneca Falls meeting somewhat amusing, especially the demand for suffrage; her father, like many Quaker men, had never exercised his right to vote due to religious principle, and so Anthony saw little value in it. She was therefore surprised to learn that her parents and her youngest sister, Mary, had attended a second women's rights convention held in Rochester on August 2, 1848, where they had signed the resolutions in support of women's rights. "Susan listened attentively to her sister's enthusiastic reports," Barry notes, "but she was not drawn to the new movement with hearty conviction." Her interests lay elsewhere, and only gradually was her curiosity roused. She did not attend any women's rights conventions, but she continued to follow the news about them, and she was particularly struck by an 1850 speech by Lucy Stone, which she read in the *New York Tribune.* She decided that she would like to meet these intriguing women and learn more about their cause.

TAKING ON A NEW CRUSADE

Anthony got her chance in May 1851, when her fellow temperance worker Amelia Bloomer invited her to Seneca Falls to attend an anti-slavery lecture. Bloomer had recently popularized a revolutionary new fashion for women, consisting of loose trousers worn under a short skirt. She also knew Elizabeth Cady Stanton through her involvement in the women's movement. Walking home after the lecture, the two women ran into Stanton, and Bloomer introduced her friends to each other. Stanton liked Anthony immediately. Over the next few months, she invited Anthony to visit her in Seneca Falls and made sure that Anthony met other leaders of the women's rights movement, including Lucy Stone, Antoinette Brown, and Lucretia Mott. Anthony found their arguments convincing, and within a year, she was attending women's rights conventions and wearing bloomers.

Anthony's primary focus was still the temperance cause, but she was growing increasingly disturbed by the treatment of women within that movement. For instance, in January 1852, she and several other members of the Daughters of Temperance attended a meeting of their brother organization, the Sons of Temperance. Anthony rose to speak to the floor, but the presiding officer refused to recognize her, saying that the women had been invited only "to listen and learn." Furious, she stormed out of the hall and began drawing up plans for a new organization, the Woman's State Temperance Society. She intended this organization to be more progressive than other temperance groups and to provide more opportunities for women's involvement. In 1853, however, Anthony lost control of the society after a takeover by conservative temperance workers. The experience convinced her that women could do little useful work in the temperance field until they obtained more political rights and social freedom.

From this point on, Anthony committed her formidable

energies to the cause of women's rights. She soon revealed herself to be a superb strategist, administrator, and field commander. Before Anthony entered the ring, the feminist movement had largely consisted of conventions in which supporters gathered to discuss the issues that concerned them. Talk was not enough for Anthony. Her natural inclination was toward action: She excelled at developing tactics, directing campaigns, raising money, motivating her comrades, and recruiting volunteers. Almost singlehandedly, she transformed what had been a relatively sedate movement into a powerful source of political agitation. Her fellow activists, impressed by her fierce determination and leadership abilities, nicknamed her "the General" and "Napoleon."

Anthony could be demanding of her recruits, but she spent much time in the trenches herself. For example, after leaving the temperance movement, she organized a petition drive designed to convince the New York legislature to expand the property rights of married women. She traveled throughout the state in the dead of winter, giving lectures and raising funds, trudging through deep snow from house to house with her petition forms and campaign literature. Until the very end of her life, she drew upon incredible physical reserves that enabled her to travel extensively and work tirelessly.

Moreover, Anthony was practically immune to criticism: She paid no mind to the countless newspaper reports that mocked her as "the typical old maid, tall, angular and inclined to be vinegar visaged." And although she eventually stopped wearing bloomers, it was not so much because of the jeers they attracted but because Anthony felt the unusual outfit drew her audience's attention away from her words. She did not mind what people thought of her personally, but she would not abide anything that lessened her effectiveness for the cause.

TURMOIL WITHIN THE MOVEMENT

By the mid-1850s, Anthony had given over farm work to concentrate fully on her burgeoning career as an activist. Her skilled management of the married women's property rights campaign came to the notice of the leaders of the American Anti-Slavery Society, who offered her a paid position as an agent. Anthony gladly accepted, with the understanding that she would still devote some of her time to women's rights. As important as she believed the women's rights movement to be, Anthony realized that the controversy over the continued existence of slavery had become the most crucial issue in the United States. She felt a sacred obligation to do whatever she could to bring this "offense in the sight of High Heaven" to an end.

When the Civil War began in the spring of 1861, Anthony and the other leaders of the women's rights movement faced an important decision: In this time of national crisis, should they continue to agitate for women's rights, or should they place the movement in hiatus for the duration of the hostilities? Anthony strongly believed that, war or no war, they could not afford to put the movement on hold. She warned that any decrease in momentum would only work against them. But none of the others agreed, and so Anthony reluctantly acquiesced to their judgment. However, Anthony and Stanton did try another tactic—in 1863, they founded the Woman's National Loyal League. The goal of this organization was to support the Union's war efforts and urge the complete emancipation of the slaves. To this end, the league sponsored an enormous petition drive, collecting nearly four hundred thousand signatures calling for passage of the Thirteenth Amendment. Through the league's wartime activities, Anthony and Stanton meant to prove that women were worthy of the right to vote. They hoped that after the war, the government would reward women's patriotic endeavors by granting them suffrage.

Their hopes were dashed only a few months after the end of the Civil War, when the U.S. Congress began deliberations on a proposed Fourteenth Amendment. The amendment was intended to protect the civil rights of African Americans, a goal that Anthony and Stanton backed. But the wording of the amendment specifically defined voters as "male"; if adopted as written, Anthony realized, it would introduce gender into the Constitution for the first time. She rushed to remobilize the feminist movement to counter this unwelcome development and proposed the establishment of an American Equal Rights Association dedicated to obtaining suffrage for all citizens, regardless of race or sex.

Unfortunately, the association was weakened from the very beginning by dissension among its members. Although all agreed on the desirability of universal suffrage, they differed over tactics and timing. Some members, including Lucy Stone, argued that they should only fight one battle at a time, shelving their demands for women's suffrage until black men's voting rights were secured. The other side balked at the suggestion that the association should support any amendments or legislation that excluded women. Anthony took the second stance: "I would sooner cut off my right hand than ask the ballot for the black man and not the woman," she declared.

The trouble worsened when Anthony and Stanton made the acquaintance of George Francis Train, an eccentric millionaire who promised to provide them with the financial backing to start a feminist newspaper. While he enthusiastically promoted women's suffrage, Train was a blatant racist who denigrated African Americans in his suffrage speeches. Stone and the other members of the first faction were horrified by Train's racist remarks and appalled that Anthony would continue to associate with him. But Anthony no longer cared what they thought. She had worked long and hard for the eradication of slavery, and now she felt that her former colleagues had betrayed her with their half-hearted dedication to women's suffrage. According to historian Geoffrey C. Ward, "Train's commitment to women's rights and his pledge of financial support were evidently enough to make her close her eyes" to his shortcomings.

The conflict finally reached the boiling point at the May 1869 meeting of the American Equal Rights Association. The topic under discussion was the proposed Fifteenth Amendment, which also specifically excluded women from the right to vote. A furious debate broke out: Personal accusations flew back and forth, bitter words were spoken. Immediately afterwards, Anthony and Stanton established a new organization, the National Woman Suffrage Association (NWSA). Stone retaliated by starting her own group, the American Woman Suffrage Association (AWSA). It was the beginning of a twenty-year split in the women's rights movement.

POLITICS AS USUAL

Anthony and the other members of NWSA were unable to convince Congress to revise the exclusionary language in the Fifteenth Amendment or to prevent its ratification by the states. Instead, they instituted a new campaign, agitating for the passage of a "Sixteenth Amendment" granting suffrage to women. The association's agenda also encompassed divorce reform, coeducation, equal pay for working women, and other related issues—some of which were considered quite radical. In this respect, NWSA differed greatly from AWSA, which focused solely on women's suffrage and whose members tended to be more conservative.

Anthony insisted that Stanton serve as the president of NWSA; for herself, she would only accept secondary titles such as the chair of the executive committee or vice president at large. Nevertheless, as Harper explains, "Anthony's organizational genius, strategic savvy, and grueling preparations in the months prior to each convention led her colleagues to acknowledge her as the principal leader" of the group. Anthony made a point of holding the annual NWSA convention in Washington, D.C.; while there, she usually managed to address a congressional committee or two, pushing for a federal suffrage amendment.

Over the years, Anthony became a regular fixture at the capitol, enlisting sympathetic senators in her cause and taking careful note of which politicians opposed the amendment. As journalist Lynn Sherr describes,

> She got so proficient, that when one committee reported unfavorably on The Cause, she polled the absent members to find out how they would have voted, tallied up the score, then reported the results to the press triumphantly to prove they could almost have won.

Anthony could be persistent to the point of annoyance. One of her staunchest supporters, Senator Henry W. Blair of New Hampshire, teased her in a letter:

> I thought just as likely as not you would come fussing round before I got your amendment reported to the Senate. I wish you would go home. . . . I don't see what you want to meddle for, anyway. Go off and get married!

Nor was she intimidated by the powerful: She buttonholed more than one president on the issue of women's rights. She badgered Andrew Johnson until he subscribed to the *Revolution*, her feminist newspaper, and she became so frustrated with Theodore Roosevelt's refusal to publicly announce his approval of women's suffrage that she told him outright, "I hope you will not be a candidate for the office again!"

Before the Civil War, Anthony had been a solid antislavery Republican, but after her Republican allies ignored her objections to the Fourteenth and Fifteenth Amendments, she looked for aid from any likely candidates. During na-

HOLD ITEM

NODSION -LO

**Take this item
to the checkout
desk or self check
machine before
you leave the
Library.**

*Thank you for visiting the
Kansas City Public Library!*

KANSAS CITY
PUBLIC
LIBRARY

Maura Perez
(Angelica)

03- 4012 664

tional elections, Professor Mary D. Pellauer writes, "she demanded a suffrage plank on the platforms of political parties of all sorts." Anthony summed up her philosophy in this manner: "We are for suffrage wherever we find it, and we shall help those who help us. After we get our right to vote we shall use it as we choose individually."

Although she favored a national suffrage amendment, whenever a state or territory held a referendum on women's right to vote, Anthony marshaled her forces into the field. Frequently she joined her coworkers on tour, canvassing the region with petitions or scheduling a staggering number of speeches. At the age of seventy-six, for instance, Anthony spent eight months traveling up and down California rallying support for the state's suffrage referendum, giving as many as three lectures a day. But she remained skeptical of the wisdom of working for suffrage on a state-by-state basis, and with good reason: By the time of her death, only four states had enfranchised women.

THE NEXT GENERATION

For most of her life, Anthony remained confident that she would see the passage of the suffrage amendment. As she reached old age, however, she admitted to herself that this seemed increasingly unlikely. Now one of her most important tasks would be to prepare the younger women in the movement to carry on after she was gone. According to Pellauer,

> More than any other activist of her generation, it was Anthony who provided the continuity of the movement. She sought out bright, articulate, promising young women . . . , nurtured their talent, and assured a generation to carry on after the feminist "pioneers."

To these young suffragists, Anthony was a hero. They called her "Aunt Susan" as a sign of their admiration and respect, and she fondly referred to them as "my girls."

Largely in consideration of this new generation, Anthony entered into negotiations concerning a proposed merger of NWSA and AWSA during the late 1880s. She understood that, however emotionally painful that conflict had been for her in 1869, it meant next to nothing to the suffragists who were too young to remember those days. Furthermore, she knew that the movement's ability to survive would be strengthened if the division was healed. On February 18, 1890, the two organizations reunited as the National American

Woman Suffrage Association (NAWSA). As always, Stanton served as president, but after her retirement in 1892, Anthony finally accepted the post.

For the next six years, Anthony continued to work as hard as ever; when worried friends suggested that she let up some on account of her age, she scoffed. "I feel young and buoyant," she announced, "and I have no concern but that when I am done working for the suffrage cause thousands of other women will go right on with the work." When she turned eighty in 1900, she resigned from the presidency of NAWSA, but only with the following caveat:

> I am not retiring now because I feel unable, mentally or physically, to do the necessary work, but because I wish to see the organization in the hands of those who are to have its management in the future. I want to see you all at work, while I am alive, so I can scold if you do not do it well.

Later that same year, though, Anthony suffered a stroke—due in large part, her doctor felt, to overwork and exhaustive travel. Several months of bedrest and recuperation followed, after which Anthony recovered her health enough to resume her constant journeying. She even crossed the ocean in 1904 to attend an international women's convention in Europe. This traveling was all done, of course, against her doctor's advice; Anthony briefly considered curtailing her trips and her political activism, but she decided she would prefer to "die in the harness" rather than give up the work that had made her life so worthwhile.

She remained active until her final illness in the winter of 1906. Intent on going to the annual NAWSA convention in Baltimore, she boarded a train in the middle of a snowstorm and soon developed a severe cold that progressed into pneumonia. She missed most of the sessions, but through sheer strength of will she managed to leave her sickbed long enough to deliver an address. Knowing that this would be her last women's rights convention, she said:

> These have been wonderful addresses and speeches I have listened to during the past week. Yet I have looked on many such audiences, and in my life time I have listened to many such speakers, all testifying to the righteousness, the justice, and the worthiness of the cause of woman suffrage. . . . Most of these who worked with me in the early years have gone on. I am here for a little time only and then my place will be filled as theirs was filled. The fight must not cease; you must see that it does not stop.

ANTHONY'S LEGACY

Amid her young coworkers, Anthony kept a positive outlook, exhorting them in brave words to complete her life's mission. But once home, confined to her bed and realizing that she would never leave it again, she allowed herself to grieve a little over what she saw as her failure. "Just think of it," she sighed, "I have been striving for over sixty years for a little bit of justice no bigger than that, and yet I must die without obtaining it. Oh, it seems so cruel!"

Anthony died at the age of eighty-six on March 13, 1906. A raging blizzard could not keep away the ten thousand mourners who gathered in Rochester for her funeral. She had touched that many lives and more, whether she realized it or not, for her tireless work and unflinching courage had radically altered the condition of women in America. Her young successors in the suffrage movement had never been barred from speaking in public. They could choose to attend any number of prestigious women's colleges or coeducational universities. More professions were open to them than ever before; at the turn of the century, the census listed women employed in jobs ranging from physicians and ministers to carpenters and blacksmiths. Married women had gained almost all of their legal rights, enjoying far greater control over their property and income. Perhaps most important of all, public attitudes toward women's rights had changed significantly. The opinions that had earned Anthony nothing but derision fifty years ago no longer seemed so strange. Then people had considered the very idea of women going to the polls to cast their votes as freakishly unnatural; by 1906, it was not difficult to imagine, especially since women in four states already voted on election day.

As Anthony had hoped, the fight for suffrage did not cease. Though it took fourteen more years, her loyal followers finally achieved their goal with the ratification of the Nineteenth Amendment in 1920. Anthony did not live to see that day, but no one could deny her importance in the winning of that shining victory, nor the immeasurable debt owed to her by the women of future generations.

ANTHONY'S EARLY YEARS: THE MAKING OF AN ACTIVIST

PEOPLE
WHO MADE
HISTORY

SUSAN B. ANTHONY

The Influence of a Liberal Quaker Upbringing

Geoffrey C. Ward

A screenwriter and historian, Geoffrey C. Ward has collaborated with the acclaimed director Ken Burns on several documentaries, including the award-winning series *The Civil War*. The following selection is excerpted from Ward's *Not for Ourselves Alone: The Story of Elizabeth Cady Stanton and Susan B. Anthony*, the companion book to the documentary film of the same name. Ward explains that Anthony was raised in a liberal Quaker household by parents who were dedicated to working for reform-minded causes such as temperance and abolitionism. In particular, he notes, Anthony's father greatly influenced her by insisting that his daughters be prepared to make their way independently in life and allowing them educational and work opportunities not often permitted to young women of their social class.

Susan B. Anthony did not share her great friend Elizabeth Cady Stanton's literary gifts. "Whenever I take my pen in hand," she confessed to her first biographer, "I always seem to be mounted on stilts." Nor did she share Stanton's fondness for drawing universal lessons from arranging and rearranging the events of her own girlhood. As an adult, she was a whirlwind, so relentlessly active that she left little time for the sort of self-examination that might have helped explain precisely how a shy, self-conscious young woman seemingly consumed with self-doubt managed within a very few years to transform herself into an utterly self-reliant political leader whose boldness matched that of any other woman of her time.

Some part of the answer—but only part—clearly lay within

the home in which she spent her first eighteen years. Elizabeth Cady Stanton's rebelliousness represented a deliberate breaking-away from a determinedly traditional household. Anthony's rebellion was no less intense, her independent spirit and willingness to go it alone in some ways still more remarkable, but both were at least in part in keeping with the traditions preached and practiced by her family. Her parents believed it was the first duty of every human being to do what he or she could to be useful to the world, a conviction they somehow managed to convey to all six of their children who survived into adulthood. Both their sons would play active roles in the Kansas struggle against slavery; both of Susan's married sisters supported her work for suffrage, while her unmarried youngest sister, Mary, would fight for it openly, often at her side.

The elder Anthonys identified early with each of the two causes to which Susan would first devote herself—temperance and abolitionism—and were entirely sympathetic when she finally fixed upon women's rights as her life's work. Although she became America's most celebrated proponent of a woman's right to remain single and completely independent, she was devoted to her family and would draw all her life on the support and encouragement of every member of it.

THE INFLUENCE OF RELIGION

Susan Brownell Anthony was born near Adams, Massachusetts, on February 15, 1820. Her father, Daniel, was a Quaker farmer so devout that toys, games, and music were all barred from his house for fear they might distract the children from what was called the Inner Light—the God who lived within every soul—and so committed to pacifism that he refused to vote or pay taxes to a government willing to wage war. When the tax collector came to call, he placed his purse on the table and said, "I shall not voluntarily pay these taxes; If thee wants to rifle my pocketbook, thee may do so." And he shared fully in the Quaker belief that men and women were equal before God; his own sister was a Quaker elder and respected preacher.

But Daniel Anthony's relationship with the Friends was never simple. He was made to apologize to the Meeting for his "misconduct" in marrying Susan's mother, Lucy Read, a Baptist; was brought before the congregation again to explain why he had dared go "out of plainness" by wearing a handsome cape purchased in New York, and was finally read out of Meeting altogether because—in order to provide local young people a place in which to learn to dance other than in taverns, where alcohol was served—he had opened up his attic as a dancing school. (The fact that he had been careful to keep his own children from taking part in the dancing did not

A SENSE OF EQUALITY

Among early American religious groups, the Quakers were unique in their egalitarian treatment of women, who were permitted to speak during services and to hold important posts. According to Alma Lutz, this matter-of-fact attitude toward women's equality had a significant impact on Anthony during her youth. Lutz was a suffragist during the 1910s and continued to work for women's rights after the passage of the Nineteenth Amendment. The following excerpt is taken from her book Susan B. Anthony: Rebel, Crusader, Humanitarian.

The Quakers' respect for women's equality with men before God left its mark on young Susan. As soon as she was old enough she went regularly to Meeting with her father. . . . Susan, sitting with the women and children on the hand-hewn benches near the big fireplace in the meeting house which her ancestors had built, found peace and consecration in the simple unordered service, in the long reverent silence broken by both the men and the women in the congregation as they were led to say a prayer or give out a helpful message. Forty families now worshiped here, the women sitting on one side and the men on the other; but women took their places with men in positions of honor, Susan's own grandmother, Hannah Latham Anthony, an elder, sitting in the "high seat," and her aunt, Hannah Anthony Hoxie, preaching as the spirit moved her. With this valuation of women accepted as a matter of course in her church and family circle, Susan took it for granted that it existed everywhere. . . .

This was Susan's heritage—Quaker discipline and austerity lightened by her father's independent spirit and by the kindly understanding of her mother who had not forgotten her own fun-loving girlhood; an environment where men and women were partners in church and at home, where hard physical work was respected, where help for the needy and unfortunate was spontaneous, and where education was regarded as so important that Grandfather Anthony built a school for his children and the neighbors' in his front yard.

Alma Lutz, *Susan B. Anthony: Rebel, Crusader, Humanitarian,* 1959.

sway the elders.) Susan inherited from her father a host of Quaker qualities—humility, austerity, egalitarianism—along with a deep distrust of orthodoxy.

Her mother was a shy, reticent woman, so modest she is said never to have so much as mentioned any of her pregnancies—Susan was the second of eight children—to a living soul other than her husband and her mother. She had given up the simplest pleasures to marry her Quaker husband—singing, dancing, brightly colored clothing—and accepted with good grace even the criticism of her husband's Quaker neighbors who overheard her humming lullabies to her babies. And when the time came, she agreed that her children should all become members of the Friends' Meeting. She herself, though, never became a Quaker, claiming always that she was "not good enough."

HARD WORK

Not long after Susan was born, her father harnessed the stream that twisted through his farm to power a small cotton mill and staffed it with young women from the surrounding hills; unlike Elizabeth Cady Stanton, who would have to develop her empathy for working-class women secondhand, Susan B. Anthony was surrounded from earliest childhood by women who earned their own livelihoods. As many as eleven mill girls sometimes boarded in the Anthony home. Lucy Read Anthony had to not only care for her own children but look after these boarders as well. She did so without complaint, but her daughters were all expected to help, and from early girlhood Susan was accustomed to an almost ceaseless round of work—sewing, cleaning, hauling water, preparing three meals a day for as many as sixteen people, and washing up again once they had finished eating. When her enemies in later years charged that because she had never married she couldn't possibly understand the supposed advantages of remaining within "woman's sphere," the memory of her mother's sacrifices and her own sometimes arduous girlhood must have made her smile.

Susan was precocious enough to have learned to read before the age of four, but she is said to have strained her eyes so badly that they crossed. The left one eventually straightened itself, but the right would remain out of alignment all her life, a source of sufficient self-consciousness that in later years she would rarely allow that side of her face to be photographed. She seems to have been unusually conscientious, too. When, at the age of eleven, she earned three dollars substituting at one of her father's looms for two weeks, she used every penny of it to buy three blue teacups for her overworked mother, and when the male foreman left and she suggested that one of the women be appointed to replace him, she was disappointed when her father said that putting a woman in charge would never do.

In 1826, Daniel Anthony moved his family to nearby Battenville, New York, built himself a handsome fifteen-room house, and began running several mills for a local businessman. By 1835 he had become one of the most important men in the community.

STUDENT AND TEACHER

Susan attended the district school until the male teacher reached long division and refused to teach it to her, either because he did not believe girls needed such lofty knowledge or because he secretly hadn't mastered it himself. In any case, her father pulled her out of the classroom and started a home school for his children and the women who worked in his mills. Daniel Anthony taught classes himself at first, then hired a series of teachers, including Mary Perkins, trained by the educational pioneer Mary Lyon. Susan was accustomed to the young women who worked in her father's mills, but Mary Perkins was different—an independent, unmarried woman who had been "fashionably educated."

Beginning in the summer of Susan's fifteenth year, Daniel Anthony saw to it that she and her older sister, Guelma, took teaching jobs themselves, first acting as governesses in the homes of family friends, then taking over classrooms in the district school at one dollar and fifty cents a week—roughly one quarter of the salary that had been paid to the men they replaced. Inequities in pay between men and women were abstractions to Elizabeth Cady Stanton; they would remain vivid memories to Susan B. Anthony.

When neighbors criticized Daniel Anthony for allowing his daughters to earn their own wages, he was unperturbed: "I am fully of the belief that shouldst thou never teach school a single day afterwards," he assured Guelma, "thou wouldst ever feel to justify thy course. . . . Thou wouldst seem to me to be laying the foundation for thy far greater usefulness."

Anthony's Traumatic Experiences at Boarding School

Kathleen Barry

In the following excerpt from her book *Susan B. Anthony: A Biography of a Singular Feminist*, Kathleen Barry explores Anthony's troubled time at a Quaker boarding school for young women. Although Anthony was eager to continue her education, Barry writes, she had never before been very far away from her family and developed an extreme case of homesickness that, despite her best efforts, she was unable to overcome. Anthony's emotional distress was heightened by constant criticism from the school's headmistress, who strove to inculcate the students with moral piety by scrutinizing their smallest faults, according to the author. In Barry's opinion, this experience deeply affected Anthony, causing her to develop a relentless drive for self-improvement that had both positive and negative effects on her personality. Barry is a professor of human development and sociology at Pennsylvania State University in University Park.

Between home and factory Daniel Anthony constructed his own paternalistic community in which he extended his care for his wife and children to his workers. . . . When Daniel organized a home school for his children, he also provided an evening school for his employees. Susan recalled that the school was in session "from eight to nine o'clock, and it was considered unpopular not to attend. Half the employees of the factory were there, learning to read and write or spell." At first, Susan's father taught the classes himself, but eventually he hired a full-time teacher who instructed the children during the day and the employees in the evening.

To find a teacher for his own school, Daniel Anthony inquired at the new female seminaries and found a young woman who had been a student of Mary Lyons. In the late 1830s in western Massachusetts, Mary Lyons had made a pioneering advance in women's education when she had founded Mount Holyoke Seminary, then the only school to provide the closest approximation to a male university education. There was no full-fledged university education for women at that time. Not until 1864, when Vassar opened as the first all-women's college, was the same level of undergraduate college education available to young women that had been offered to men since the founding of Harvard in 1636. Mount Holyoke did not begin as a woman's college but it was the first endowed seminary for young women that made it possible for girls from all social classes to take advantage of a higher level of education, as entrance was not dependent on their ability to pay. But before her dream of Mount Holyoke had come to fruition, Mary Lyons had taught at Ipswich Academy in Massachusetts, and one of her students there had been Mary Perkins.

After she finished her studies, Daniel Anthony hired Mary Perkins to teach in his school. The community found it very impressive that he had brought such a "fashionably educated" teacher to their "modern" school. . . .

Mary Perkins offered a new image of womanhood to Susan and her sisters. She was independent and educated; as a teacher, she held a position that had been traditionally reserved to young men graduating from universities and theological seminaries. . . .

It was not long before Susan became aware of the limits of her own education in their home school. When her father saw how much she loved school and her eagerness to continue, he began to inquire about an appropriate Quaker boarding school for his daughters. He found a suitable school, Deborah Moulson's Female Seminary, far away in Hamilton, Pennsylvania, outside of Philadelphia. But just as he was ready to enroll his daughters, his business began to plunge during the panic of 1837.

ECONOMIC HARDSHIPS

The early 1830s had been a time of rapid economic expansion in the United States. The new mills and factories generated a profitable trade, both foreign and domestic commerce were thriving, the value of real estate rose, and there was no absence of money in the economy. But this optimistic economy stood on shaky ground. As property values rose, over-trading and restless—if not reckless—investing threatened the economy. Then President Andrew Jackson decided to close the Bank of the United States, causing a rapid downward spiral in the economy. This bank, originally chartered in 1816, was to be rechartered by 1836. But Andrew Jackson, who distrusted banks and did not understand their function, argued that monied interests, merchants, financiers, and paper money were the enemies of the common man. He prevented the bank from being rechartered, dismantled it, and arranged for the federal government's deposits to be made in state banks. At the same time, the government tried to institute specie payments and began to accept gold and silver for the sale of public lands, which was at an all-time high with the settlement of the West. A wildly fluctuating currency resulted and forced the withdrawal of specie payments. Coins became rare and were hoarded, which consequently provoked counterfeiting. These problems, along with overproduction—particularly of cotton—and high speculation on the market, accelerated the economic crisis and finally brought the country into a deep depression, the panic of 1837.

Daniel sent his eldest daughter, Guelma, away to the seminary first; but later that year he told his brother that "there is none to pay her tuition bills. . . . It seems inevitable now that my business is likely to turn out most miserably." But Deborah Moulson offered Guelma a position as a teaching assistant, which allowed her to stay in school. Daniel cautioned his daughter that "cash in this country is scarce, the best of economy in the use of it will be highly necessary, thy mother advises nothing but except what stern necessity calls aloud for."

Caution began to mark all of the Anthony family's life. But in regard to the children's education, Daniel and Lucy strictly observed Quaker leader William Penn's advice to "spare no cost for by such parsimony all is lost that is saved." When Guelma became ambivalent about staying on at school for a second term, Daniel told her that this "opportunity for study and improvement in many branches should be taken seriously, when I consider that this most likely will be the last opportunity thou will ever have of acquiring information of the kind much needed by all before commencing life and being absorbed in the cares thereof." By the end of the year, with the few resources he had left, Daniel enrolled Susan in Deborah Moulson's seminary, somehow managing to pay the 125-dollar tuition when it became clear that there was no way she could work her way through as a teaching assistant as had Guelma.

Unlike her gifted future friend Elizabeth Cady, Susan B. Anthony could not be particular about her education. Susan did not question at all going to a girls' seminary, nor did she wonder whether her education would be inferior to the education that boys were receiving in college. She was glad to have the opportunity and thought it should be made available to all girls. At her young age she had come to believe that the publicly supported district schools were lax in teaching the feminine morality of humility and piety. She, like her mother before her, had already internalized the most constraining and traditional of womanly values. She once wrote home from Hamilton: "I regret that Brothers and Sisters have not the privilege of attending a school better adapted to improvement, both in Science and Morality; surely a District School (unless they have recently reformed) is not an appropriate place for the cultivation of the latter."

Contrary to Susan's reaction to the female seminary, her future friend Elizabeth Cady was furious when she learned that she could not go off to Union College with her male classmates where she had counted on being able to continue her classical education. But that was reserved for boys. Instead, she was destined for Mrs. Emma Willard's Troy Female Seminary, where she would be seriously educated but not with the rigor of the classics. Even though Troy Female Seminary was the most prestigious education a father could offer his daughter in the 1830s and even though she worshiped Mrs. Willard, Elizabeth Cady was furious and frustrated. By the time Susan B. Anthony began her one and only term at Deborah Moulson's academy, Elizabeth had already graduated from Troy.

Deborah Moulson had advertised her female seminary with a flier in which she declared its purpose. "The inculcation of the principles of Humility, Morality and love of Virtue will receive particular attention." Even though Susan studied "Arithmetic, Algebra, Literature, Chemistry, Philosophy, Physiology and Bookkeeping," Deborah's main emphasis was "improvement in morality." Her discipline was severe and with it she cultivated the most moralistic piety of those times, which was meant to fashion the true woman.

HOMESICKNESS

Susan valued highly the opportunity to advance her education—as she put it—but more than anything Susan was a homebound young girl who at fourteen had written:

> What so sweet—
> So beautiful on earth, and oh! so rare
> As kindred love and family repose.
>
> The busy world
> With all the tumult and the stir of life,
> Pursues its wanton course; on pleasure some,
> And some on happiness; while each one loves
> One little spot in which her heart unfolds
> With nature's holiest feelings; one sweet spot,
> And calls it *Home!* If sorrow is felt there
> It runs through many bosoms, and a smile
> Lights upon in kindred eyes a smile
> And if disease intrudes, the sufferer finds
> Rest on the breast beloved.

Going to Deborah Moulson's seminary proved to be a wrenching experience for Susan. Her father accompanied her to Hamilton, and took her and Guelma sightseeing in Philadelphia, but when it was time for him to leave, Susan's reaction was intense and a bit dramatic: "O what pangs were felt, it seemed impossible for me to part with him, I could not speak to bid him Farewell."

Daniel was sure that this was childish homesickness and it would pass quickly. He wrote to his daughters while en route to Battenville: "I suppose Susan by this time has lost sight of home having had the whole day to become interested in all absorbing topicks [sic] of Hamiltonville." But Susan's anguish did not pass. A few days later, crying even while she was writing to her father, she tried to reassure him that "I was ready on the ensuing morning to commence my studies. Do not suppose I carry a gloomy countenance all the time." But a week later, "300 miles from the beloved spot, separated from all that is dear to me, excepting my elder sister," she still could not shake off her homesickness. Every time she thought of her father's departure, it "cast a gloom over my mind" and "I felt as if I could not contain myself."

Going away to school forced her to separate herself from home, to make new friends, to shoulder new responsibilities, and to enter a different social world which required new loyalties and confidences from her. She resisted! Stubbornly she proclaimed that she was in exile from her "Native Land." With no little amount of drama, she worried that this exile could be permanent. "Home! that inestimable spot is far distant," she confided to her diary. "O may I be permitted to return once and mingle with those dear Friends of my youth."

FIGHTING HER EMOTIONS

This was more than a child's usual homesickness. Susan was seventeen, approaching adulthood, and in deep emotional turmoil for probably the first time in her life. She had been a serious child. But now she was intense—deeply so, passionately so. She had no other object for the expression of her feelings than her home and family. So she focused her intensity there. Then she became rigorous with herself; each day she tried to console herself with self-rectifying thoughts. "A few moments of painful separation from friends, is but the improvement of my mind, and I ought to be content." But her emotional reactions still seemed to her to be beyond her control and that alone intensified their effect on her. When she was at home, she had focused her powerful feelings on her family. Now this sensitive and intense young woman, away at school, was lost and without focus.

Sometimes she withdrew herself from her friends at school and walked alone, while other girls played and talked together. Often she spent long hours curled up in the window seat of her room writing long letters home. Susan became depressed, not so much from missing home, although that may have triggered it, but because, like most girls of her time, she had no focus for her energy, her drive, her developing passions. Girls did not think about or plan for their future; but without this kind of self-definition, Susan was lost and for comfort anchored herself emotionally even more insistently in her family life in Battenville.

Ultimately, the practical necessity of study impressed itself upon her.

> This cloud I anticipate will soon be expelled, at least were it to continue I should be able to make but small progress in my literary pursuits. Oft times when in the act of committing lessons to memory, will all the enduring allurements of home rush upon my mind, and surely it required all the fortitude that I can command to overcome such feelings but they

must be conquered or otherwise my mind would be wholly unfit for study.

Something of her mother's self-discipline, occasioned by Lucy's own experience of Quaker morality early in her marriage, became evident in Susan. School work became a way to regain emotional control because it drew her out of herself and these depressive moods. This began what would become a life-long emotional strategy for Susan. At this young age, she was teaching herself to funnel her emotional intensity into her school work. Eventually, her work would become the expression of her intensity and her passion.

Yet there were joyful moments at the seminary. "Nature, how bounteous, how varied are thy works," she exclaimed on a field trip to the Academy of Arts and Sciences. "Numerous specimens of the mineral kingdom were exhibited. Animals and the shell tribes. On beholding them I was ready to exclaim 'O Miracle of Miracles' with the celebrated naturalist when speaking of the metamorphoses of insects." But a short time later she confessed that while studying a physiology lesson, "I indulged a little in my natural unpleasant feelings in the forepart of the evening." The trouble with her eyes compounded all these difficulties. "My eyes held in performing

Lucretia Mott

their wanted office. [But] often do their nonconformance mortify this frail heart, when attempting to read in class."

ALWAYS IN TROUBLE

Deborah Moulson did not often appear in school during the classes, but when she did it was a momentous occasion for the girls. One day when she walked into the classroom unexpectedly, Susan rushed to her and in a burst of enthusiastic pride presented her with the exercise she had just completed. Deborah stiffened, scorned Susan's paper, and without looking at the young girl said, "Obviously Susan, you do not know the rule for dotting 'i's.'" Susan was crushed. It took all the self-discipline she had to hold back her tears. She looked down and admitted, "I do not know the rule." Deborah, who obviously was in ill health, looked over the class and then turned to Susan and said, "It is no wonder I have undergone so much distress in both mind and body. I have devoted my time to you in vain." Susan now saw that she was the cause of Deborah's illness and could barely hold back her tears until the end of class, when she ran first to the privy and then to her bed to cry her heart out.

Deborah Moulson's pedagogy, a replication of guilt-laden Puritanism, oriented as it was to cultivating feminine piety, engaged her students in almost endless self-examination over the smallest infraction of her rules and the most trivial displays of pride. Susan took every admonition to heart. Although Deborah's demands for humility diverted Susan from her preoccupation with home, the consequences were often mortifying. One day Deborah reproved the girls for their moral laxity, which she said was apparent in their inattentiveness to housekeeping. In response, Susan decided to clean the schoolroom before class. She took off her shoes, climbed on top of the desks, and began to sweep away the cobwebs from the corners of the ceiling. "After going around the room, I stepped on D's desk, that I might sweep in that part, thoughtlessly, and strained the lock, bent the hinges and how much more damage I do not know." At that moment, the teaching assistant came in followed by the other girls. A tense silence gripped the air. Dutifully, the teaching assistant left the room to inform Deborah.

When Deborah arrived, Susan immediately came forth and made a full confession. "Deborah, see what I have done. I have broken your desk." Deborah ignored her. In Deborah's eyes, the road to piety and humility could not be walked that easily; experiencing humility was more important than merely admitting to an error. Susan must be made to feel it. Deborah walked slowly to her desk, inspected it, and then, as if Susan had said nothing to her, turned away from her and asked the other girls in the room who had broken her desk. Susan knew that she must remain silent; this was to be a lesson in humility. "It was Susan B. Anthony," several of the girls said.

Deborah turned to Susan and glared, "How did you come to step upon it." By this time, Susan was "too full to answer" and holding back the tears was almost impossible. Deborah turned away, leaving Susan with her humiliation. Now Susan knew that she was evil; she worried that she would never succeed in improving in morality, and that she could never overcome her evilness with piety and humility. In her old age, Susan recalled this incident while talking with her original biographer, Ida Harper, and remembered that "not once in all the sixty years that have passed, has the thought of that come to my mind without making me turn cold and sick at heart."

LEARNING FEMALE MORALITY

Being pious about small incidents made the girls feel moral or at least that they were trying to be moral. That was the essence of female morality at this time. It focused on the insignificant, the trivial and made them meaningful with heightened emotionality. The girls' conversations with each other at the Seminary were preoccupied with questions about such subjects as "feminine delicacy." In one such discussion, Susan confided to her friend Lydia Mott, Lucretia Mott's niece, "Lydia, sometimes I feel as if I were the worst girl of all being." Lydia hastily assured her that "you are right to think so. But Susan, do not give up in discouragement." These conversations and the reprimands that preceded them stimulated endless self-examination. The less specific the offense the more vague the feelings of wrongdoing and the more personally intense were the girls' self-reflection and efforts to correct the error of their ways. Personal, private morality was meant to be the all-absorbing work of the private sphere. One day when Deborah reprimanded the girls for "levity and mirthfulness," likening them to the traitor Judas Iscariot, Susan first rejected the charge, but as she thought it over, she finally concluded that "I cannot see my own defects because my heart is hardened."

This was how young girls learned to be true women in the 1830s. Although Deborah's was a Quaker boarding school, it cultivated the same guilt-inducing private piety that the early Puritan fathers had used to rule over the faithful of seventeenth-century New England. Ironically, it was the same piety that George Fox had rejected in founding the Quakers. And like the women who had been subjected to the more severe rigors of Puritanism in Anne Hutchinson's time, the impressionable young girls at Deborah's seminary often became anxious and then depressed with the seeming futility of their search for the correct path to humility and God.

Many young girls simply succumbed to this training, absorbed it, and went on with their lives. Susan's sister Guelma seems to have responded in this way. But Susan's reaction was different. First anxious, sometimes depressed, she ultimately took on this code. Her emotional intensity was focused but not subdued by Deborah's discipline.

Unlike most of the other girls, achieving piety was a challenge for Susan, and one she took up with rigor. She struggled with it. She searched within herself, disciplined herself, and eventually began to formulate her own values. It was a rough course. For better or worse, it was capable of cultivating tough—as well as true—women.

Sometime after she had left school, a dream prompted Susan to reprimand her youngest sister, twelve-year-old Mary. In Susan's dream Mary appeared sulky, and when a request was made of her she hesitated to respond. Susan interpreted her dream as an omen that showed her that she was to guide her sister away from evil ways in the manner that Deborah had guided her. She confronted Mary with her dream and asked, "Is not this dream too frequently verified in your daily conduct toward those who ask favors of you?" Mary hung her head. Susan instructed Mary not to use the handkerchief Susan had given her as a gift until she had corrected this fault.

> Rest assured Dear Sister that we all regard you equally with the rest, but that particular trait in your character, we do so dislike, and sincerely hope you may be enabled to command strength to overpower it, and thus secure your own happiness as well as those around you. Do not indulge anger toward any one, for that will also make you unhappy. Suffer yourself to think much about serious things and Death, for that will strengthen you in doing well.

Having internalized the values of true womanhood—this personalized moralistic piety—Susan was in a position to impose these values on others. She started with the youngest and weakest. Nevertheless, however negative and moralistic female seminary education was, it did encourage young women to think and act on their own. Even if their actions resulted from values imposed upon them, the point is that they *acted* and did so outside of their family context. That was more than Susan's mother had been able to do. In this fashion, female seminaries actually created a social space outside of the private sphere, where women could experiment—even in limited ways—with creating their own identity. This social space, available to young women collectively for the first time since Emma Willard had initiated her "experiment" in 1821, eventually created some of the conditions that would make it possible for women to originate their own movement.

A DIFFERENT ROLE MODEL

Not all was moralistic piety at Deborah Moulson's seminary. Lucretia Mott, the famous and controversial Quaker abolitionist, came to the school to speak to the girls on the importance of improving their intellect. A few years earlier, she had organized the Philadelphia Female Anti-Slavery Society when she found that William Lloyd Garrison's newly organized American Anti-Slavery Society was, at best, conflicted over the role women could play in it. Lucretia Mott was a different role model for the young girls, and Susan listened to her with rapt attention.

Lucretia Mott was modest but not self-deprecating; she was wise yet not intellectually ostentatious. She did not indulge herself in the petty attitudes that characterized personal piety. Instead, based on the original spirit of the Quakers, her moral convictions took the form of social and civil responsibility. Yet the distinction between morality based on civil responsibility and morality derived from personal piety was blurred in the girls' seminary training. As a result, these very different kinds of morality were made to appear as if they were the same. Mott's civil responsibility and Moulson's piety would remain undifferentiated for several years for Susan B. Anthony following her time at Deborah Moulson's academy. She would learn to make these distinctions and transform her morality only with considerable personal struggle. It would be a struggle that was unavoidable once she had embarked on a course of political leadership.

The Temperance Movement: Anthony's First Crusade

Miriam Gurko

Susan B. Anthony's career as a reformer began in the temperance movement, which sought to decrease alcoholism, promote teetotaling, and prohibit the sale and use of alcoholic beverages. This reform movement was closely tied to improving the condition of women, since wives had little protection or legal recourse against alcoholic husbands who were abusive or negligent. However, as Anthony soon discovered, female temperance workers also possessed few rights: No matter how hard they worked for the cause, they were not allowed to speak at temperance meetings or take part in the official proceedings. In the following selection from *The Ladies of Seneca Falls: The Birth of the Woman's Rights Movement,* author Miriam Gurko recounts several instances of sexism within the temperance movement that eventually convinced Anthony to devote her energies to women's rights instead.

Lucretia Mott, Martha Wright, and Lucy Stone, along with dozens of others who became involved after that first convention, all made immense contributions to woman's rights. But the driving force, the inspirational center, was provided by Elizabeth Stanton and Susan B. Anthony. Mrs. Stanton articulated the goals, Miss Anthony supplied the organizational skill and the unremitting energy which powered the movement for the next fifty years. Unitarian minister and reformer William Henry Channing called her the Napoleon of the woman's rights movement.

In 1851, when she first met Elizabeth Stanton, Susan Anthony was still primarily concerned with temperance. But her experience during the next two years not only drew her away from temperance to woman's rights, but made her realize that without those rights women could do very little for any reform. These were also the years in which she first became a public figure, and in which she found the chief purpose of her life.

BEING SILENCED

At the beginning of 1852 she was sent as a delegate from the Rochester Daughters of Temperance to a mass meeting of temperance workers held in Albany, New York, by the Sons of Temperance. The women delegates had been accepted and given seats, but when Susan Anthony rose to speak on a motion, the presiding officer stopped her. "The sisters were not invited to speak," he announced, "but to listen and learn."

She immediately walked out of the hall, followed by three or four other women. The rest of the female delegates, disapproving of these "bold, meddlesome disturbers," remained and were obediently silent during the rest of the convention.

The "bold disturbers" held their own meeting, at which they decided to form a state organization for women in which they would be free to speak and act. Susan Anthony was appointed chairman of a committee to arrange a Woman's State Temperance Convention to be held in Rochester, New York, in April 1852.

She appealed to Elizabeth Stanton for help. Mrs. Stanton was for temperance, largely because women had no legal protection against the often brutal or irresponsible behavior of alcoholic husbands. She would have preferred to see women work directly to secure legal protection, but she knew that many women were not yet ready for this. Temperance work, though secondary in her view, would at least provide them with experience and self-confidence, and bring them closer to the movement for woman's rights.

She agreed to attend and deliver a speech at the convention, though she warned Susan Anthony that what she had to say would be quite radical. By now she was more than ever incensed at the position of women, at the church as "a terrible engine of oppression . . . as concerns woman," and at the refusal of men to permit women to speak at conventions. "I am at the boiling point!" she wrote to Susan Anthony. "If I do not find some day the use of my tongue on this question, I shall die of an intellectual repression, a woman's rights convulsion!"

At the convention a permanent organization, the Woman's State Temperance Society, was set up, with Mrs. Stanton as president, Susan Anthony and Amelia Bloomer as secretaries. In her speech, Mrs. Stanton made an astonishing proposal. "Let no woman," she declared, "remain in the relation of wife with the confirmed drunkard. Let no drunkard be the father of her children." The state laws, she continued, should be changed so that "the drunkard shall have no claims on either wife or child."

This open advocacy of divorce plainly disconcerted her conservative listeners. Her remarks seemed even more outrageous coming from a woman wearing the immodest bloomer costume, with her hair cut short. Short hair was not uncommon for women at the time; but, combined with bloomers, it heightened the impression of defiant unconventionality. Men and women alike criticized her severely. Both press and pulpit strongly condemned the "radical Mrs. Stanton."

In June, while reaction to Mrs. Stanton was still strong, the Men's State Temperance Society held a convention in Syracuse. All temperance groups were invited to send delegates. The newly formed Woman's State Temperance Society chose Susan Anthony and Amelia Bloomer. When they arrived, both wearing bloomer dresses and Susan with her hair cut short, the clergymen who formed the majority of those present were indignant. Many threatened to leave if such unseemly females were admitted. But the ladies were allowed to enter the hall, and the convention began. When the secretary closed his annual report by welcoming the formation of the Woman's Temperance Society, one of the ministers burst out with a furious and almost hysterical speech. He fiercely opposed any recognition of the new woman's society, saying its members were a "hybrid species, half man and half woman, belonging to neither sex." This society and the woman's rights movement "must be put down, cut up root and branch."

At this, the whole convention broke into an uproar. There were angry arguments over whether the female delegates should be allowed to take part in the proceedings. A few of the male delegates tried to defend the women, but were shouted down. Only once did a woman, Susan Anthony, try to speak. There were cries of "Hear the lady!"

"Let her speak!" and even louder cries of "Never! Never!" She was ruled out of order and peremptorily told to sit down. The debate raged for the rest of the session, with the women remaining silent. At the end, the president ruled against them. Though they had been invited, they would not be allowed to participate.

THE LINK BETWEEN TEMPERANCE AND WOMEN'S RIGHTS

A retired history professor from Dartmouth College in Hanover, New Hampshire, Robert E. Riegel is the author of several books, including American Women: A Story of Social Change *and* American Feminists, *from which the following passage is taken. Riegel discusses the ways in which Anthony linked the causes of temperance and women's rights in her early speeches on temperance.*

Miss Anthony's work of the early 1850's stressed temperance more than women's rights, but the two were closely connected. The common assumption of all temperance advocates, including Miss Anthony, was that practically all the drunkards were men and all the sufferers women. Every possible ounce of pathos was utilized in picturing the terrible plight of the poor wife and mother without legal recourse who was mistreated by a drunken brute of a husband. Miss Anthony went so far as to insist that such an unfortunate wife should refuse to have children by her disreputable husband, whereupon the newspapers expressed shocked horror that a presumably chaste maiden lady should discuss the intimacies of married life. Possibly they felt that such a lady, even if she no longer believed in the stork, should not admit her lapse from perfect innocence. At any rate, temperance speeches such as those of Miss Anthony made perfectly clear that women were more moral than men and that giving them the vote would hasten the day of state prohibitory laws.

Robert E. Riegel, *American Feminists*, 1963.

It was very like what had happened at the World Anti-Slavery Convention in 1840, which had convinced Lucretia Mott and Elizabeth Stanton of the need for a woman's rights movement. Susan Anthony, sitting in enforced silence as they had done, felt the same anger and chagrin. Now she too was convinced that before she could work for any reform, she must first overcome the handicap of being a woman. And the best way to do this was to yield to Mrs. Stanton's urgings and transfer her energies to the woman's rights movement. . . .

A CONSERVATIVE BACKLASH

For a short time after the convention, Susan Anthony continued to work for temperance. With Amelia Bloomer she traveled through New York State in the spring of 1853, giving temperance lectures. But her original impetus was gone; she now considered temperance a lesser reform. More and more in her talks she stressed, not the generalized virtues of temperance, but the specific problems of women whose marriages were unhappily affected by their husbands' drinking. The way to handle these problems, she said, was to give women the right to divorce alcoholic husbands, the right to keep their own earnings, and, above all, the right to vote for these rights, which men would not, of their own volition, give to women.

Elizabeth Stanton, as president of the Woman's State Temperance Society, was also emphasizing the need for gaining these rights before women could do much about temperance. By the time the first annual convention of the society was held in June 1853, at Rochester, both Mrs. Stanton and Miss Anthony had stirred up a good deal of opposition among the more conservative members. . . .

Mrs. Stanton's emphasis on woman's rights was regarded by some women as altogether too radical. They were shocked at her support of divorce on the grounds of drunkenness; they were offended by her attack on the church for its subjection of women. They would have liked to depose her as president of the Woman's State Temperance Society, but they were in the minority and by themselves could do nothing.

They could, however, push through an amendment to the society's constitution which would allow men to participate as full members. Mrs. Stanton was strongly opposed, saying men would take control, which is exactly what they did. Once the men had been accepted, they demanded that the organization have nothing to do with woman's rights. They also printed an opposition ticket, which defeated Mrs. Stanton as president by three votes. She was elected vice president instead, and Susan Anthony reelected secretary; but they refused to serve and resigned from the organization. . . .

Susan Anthony was distressed over what amounted to a

defeat of the progressive forces in the woman's temperance movement; but Elizabeth Stanton was, if anything, relieved. Now she could devote all her efforts to woman's rights. She wrote to Susan Anthony: "Now, Susan, I do beg of you . . . to waste no more powder on the Woman's State Temperance Society. We have other and bigger fish to fry."

THE FINAL STRAW

Susan Anthony was at last ready to give up temperance work, but there was still a tag end to clear away.

In September of that year, 1853, New York City broke out in a rash of special activities. There were two temperance conventions, an antislavery convention, a woman's rights convention, and the first world's fair to be held in the United States. The first temperance convention and the antislavery meeting passed off without incident, but the second temperance convention ran into trouble.

It started when the Reverend Antoinette Brown, an accredited delegate, tried to speak. She stood on the platform for an hour and a half while a violent argument raged over the propriety of a woman speaking. One minister kept shouting, "Shame on the woman!" Others called out, "She shan't speak!" In the end, she had to leave the hall. The argument continued for three days, with Susan Anthony—who was also a delegate—listening but unable to take any part. The final decision was against women, but Miss Anthony had also come to a decision: if it took her whole lifetime, she resolved, she would never rest until women had the right to speak freely at any public gathering, on any subject.

Anthony's Career as an Abolitionist

Katharine Anthony

Distantly related to Susan B. Anthony, author Katharine Anthony is known for her best-selling biographies of history's notable women, including *Catherine the Great, Louisa May Alcott, Dolly Madison: Her Life and Times, Margaret Fuller: A Psychological Biography,* and *First Lady of the Revolution: The Life of Mercy Otis Warren.* The following selection is taken from her book *Susan B. Anthony: Her Personal History and Her Era.* According to the author, Susan B. Anthony's brief career as a paid agent of the American Anti-Slavery Society was crucial in her development as a lecturer and campaign organizer—skills that she would later employ for the cause of women's rights.

From the beginning the Abolitionists welcomed women into the fighting ranks. Among the earliest leaders were Angelina and Sarah Grimké, who had freed their slaves and left their South Carolina home to preach the gospel of emancipation in the North. The women of Boston, led by Maria Chapman, Lydia Maria Child, and Elizabeth Peabody, wrote for the press, held fairs to raise money, and spoke in public for the cause. Abby Kelly, the Quaker schoolmistress, abandoned teaching to become one of the first missionaries of the American Anti-Slavery Society. As a testimonial to the women's efforts, William Lloyd Garrison had chosen to sit out the World Anti-Slavery Convention in the woman's gallery when they were banished from the floor.

JOINING THE ABOLITIONISTS

Abby Kelley, who married her co-worker, Stephen S. Foster, was among the first women speakers who came under Su-

From *Susan B. Anthony: Her Personal History and Her Era,* by Katharine Anthony. Copyright © 1954 by Katharine Anthony. Used by permission of Doubleday, a division of Random House, Inc.

san B. Anthony's ken. Susan had just returned home from
Canajoharie, New York [after resigning from her position as
headmistress of the Canajoharie Academy] when the Fosters
arrived in Rochester for a week's campaign in the neighbor-
hood. Susan accompanied Abby Foster on her round of
meetings. Abby still had some of the old Quaker "ranting" in
her style of oratory, and this was in no wise diminished by
the opposition she encountered on this early tour.

Susan was greatly impressed by Abby Foster, whose fiery
periods awakened echoes in her own ancestral Quaker
blood. She did not join the Abolitionist forces at once, though
urged by Abby Foster to do so. But for the next five years,
while working for temperance and woman's rights, she was
moving toward her ideal of "the sublime height where now
stand Garrison, [Wendell] Phillips and all that small but noble band whose motto is 'No union with slaveholders.'" She
saw the Abolitionists as the elite of all the reformers of the
hour, partly because of the genius of their leaders and partly
because of the unstinted support they gave to the woman's
rights cause.

In September 1855, she met the leading lights of Garrison's society and was seen and noted by them. As a result
she became an agent of the American Anti-Slavery Society,
holding a position on a par with that formerly held by Henry
B. Stanton. On January 1, 1856, she received a formal letter
from the secretary of the Anti-Slavery Society offering her a
position, to begin at once and continue until May. Susan had
already arranged a tour of lectures for the woman's property
rights bill, and the dates were fixed. She could not accept at
once. The offer was postponed and renewed in October
1856, just before President James Buchanan's election and
his administration, which forced the anti-slavery issue into
a fighting cause.

She was faced by a hard winter. The political climate was
also against her. The opposition of both parties—the Democrats and the newly formed Republicans—was strong. Garrison's group demanded nothing less than immediate and
unconditional emancipation, and no political party in the
country stood for it. Susan also faced a hard life as an organizer. Her speakers developed chills, fevers, and domestic
emergencies, so that she herself, engaged up to the hilt, had
to replace them. The secretary of the society wrote her: "We
sympathize in all your trials and hope that fairer skies will

be over your head before long. Garrison says, 'Give my love to Susan, and tell her I will do for her what I would hardly do for anybody else' ... You must be dictator to all the agents in New York; when you say, 'Go,' they must go, or 'Come,' they must come, or 'Do this,' they must do it. I see no other way of getting along, and I am sure that to your gentle and wholesome rule they will cheerfully defer." Many of Susan's speakers had served on the Abolitionist platform longer than she and had no intention of deferring to her or to anyone else. Still, she managed. She had her reward when the secretary wrote her in the spring, "We have made the following a committee of arrangements for the annual meeting: Garrison, Phillips, Edmund Quincy, [Oliver] Johnson, and Susan B. Anthony." To sit on the national committee with these famous Abolitionist leaders was an honor which Susan up to now would never have dreamed of.

Her anti-slavery work had brought her recognition and had introduced other changes in her life. For the first time since leaving schoolteaching she had achieved a regularly paid salary. This amounted to ten dollars a week and her expenses. She could manage on this because she still wore her old Canajoharie dresses, toned down, turned, dyed, made over, and matched for worn spots. Ten dollars a week was more than she had ever received as a teacher, and it gave her a renewed feeling of financial independence.

Angelina Grimké

When Florence Nightingale, Susan's contemporary in England, was endowed at a similar age with an independent income by her father, it represented a great turning point in her life. Susan, with her salary, and Miss Nightingale, with her allowance, both felt they had achieved financial independence and the self-determination that this brings. Though the income was not adequate for their needs, it was an epoch-making experience in both their lives. In those days, when financial independence was rare for a single woman, the psychological effect of money she could call her own was nothing less than liberation. In their middle thirties, Susan and Florence Nightingale, thus emancipated, became conscious of great aims.

A short while later Susan wrote: "I cannot bear to make myself dependent upon relatives for the food I eat and the clothes I wear; I have never done it and hope I may never have to," and still later she declared: "No genuine equality, no real freedom, no true manhood or womanhood can exist on any foundation save that of pecuniary independence." Susan was only comparatively independent but apparently unconscious of it when the slack was taken up by her devoted and dedicated Abolitionist father. In fact, as far as the farm was concerned, Susan probably paid her way in those days when woman's labor was at a premium. She always put in her time at home working as hard as a hired servant.

A PASSIONATE SPEAKER

The second epoch-making change wrought by her anti-slavery work concerned her public speaking. In 1857 she threw away her manuscript and learned to speak from notes. She felt so strongly about human slavery that she could not bear to be tied down in speaking of the evil. As might be expected, she took her pattern from Abby Kelley Foster and declaimed rather violently. But it got her away from depending on her manuscript.

The Abolitionists were like the colonial rebels in one respect: it was easier to see King George as a tyrant because he lived in a faraway country; the Southern slaveholders were likewise tyrants far removed from sight. The Abolitionists did not care in the least if the South wanted to fly off by itself and stay there. Garrison thought it might be a good idea. When Susan inveighed against slavery she was lashing a country that was not her own. In after years she became extremely national-minded, but never in her whole lifetime did she learn to see the South as a part of the nation to which she belonged.

Once at a Quaker meeting in Easton, New York, she encountered a Virginia Quaker who undertook to apologize for slavery in his state. "Christ was no agitator, but a peacemaker," he said; "George Fox [the founder of the Quakers] was no agitator; the Friends at the South followed these examples and are never disturbed by fanaticism." Susan was horrified to hear such words proceeding from another Quaker. She was instantly on her feet and she heard herself saying: "'I came into this world not to bring peace but a sword. . . . Woe unto you, scribes and Pharisees, hypocrites that devour widows' houses!' Read the New Testament, and say if Christ was not an agitator! Who is this among us crying, 'Peace, peace, when there is no peace?'"

Only one written speech survives from the hundreds she made during her Abolitionist crusade. This sets down in black and white the passionate words that were usually extemporaneous—scathing attacks upon "the arrogant usurpers of the South," "the bloated self-conceit of traitors and rebels," and the "Hydra-Monster which sucks its life-blood from the unpaid and unpitied toil of the slaves." In the midst of her tirades she would suddenly become Susan again—the Susan to whom common sense was always the last and greatest refuge. Here is a passage from the one preserved manuscript:

> But if you emancipate the slaves, What will you do with them? What will the black man do with himself, is the question for him to answer. I am yet to learn that the Saxon man is the great reservoir of human rights to be doled out at his discretion to the nations of the earth.
>
> Do with the Negroes? What arrogance in us to put the question! What shall we do with a race of men and women who have fed, clothed, and supported both themselves and their oppressors for centuries. *Do* for the slaves? Why, allow them to do for us what they are now doing for [Southern politician and plantation owner] Jeff Davis. . . .

When her Abolitionist work ended and she returned to woman's rights, she seldom flamed with the same fierce indignation. But also she never returned to her former dependence on the pedestrian manuscript. Though speaking with a lesser heat, she could forge her sentences from a naked mind, standing in front of a listening crowd.

CHAPTER **2**

THE LEADER OF THE WOMEN'S RIGHTS MOVEMENT

PEOPLE
WHO MADE
HISTORY

SUSAN B. ANTHONY

Taking Charge of the Women's Rights Movement

Rheta Childe Dorr

At the age of twelve, Rheta Childe Dorr secretly attended a women's rights meeting despite her parents' objections. There she heard both Susan B. Anthony and Elizabeth Cady Stanton for the first time and was converted to the cause of women's suffrage on the spot. In the 1890s, Dorr embarked on a career in journalism; she also became active in the women's rights movement and founded a weekly journal called the *Suffragist*. As a foreign correspondent for the *New York Evening Mail*, she covered the communist revolution in Russia and World War I from France—dangerous jobs that were unusual for female reporters of her time.

In the following selection from her book *Susan B. Anthony: The Woman Who Changed the Mind of a Nation*, Dorr examines Anthony's assumption of the command of the women's rights movement. Unlike most of the early feminists, Dorr writes, Anthony was not content with merely discussing the issues, but was instead driven to a flurry of action and political agitation. The author observes that Anthony's tactical genius, her superb organizational skills, and her physical resilience are all apparent in her first campaign, which focused on improving the property rights of married women in the state of New York.

Up to the day and year when Susan B. Anthony assumed its direction the woman's rights movement had been limited to propaganda, widely diffused through lectures, pamphlets, newspaper discussions, pulpit fulminations, and especially through conventions, state and national. The idea of woman's rights was of course no new thing. Mary Wollstonecraft's epoch-making book, *A Vindication of the Rights of Women*, was published in 1792, and . . . made a profound impression, not only in England but in His Majesty's lately rebellious colonies where, some years before, certain ladies had brought the subject up. At least, Abigail Adams was annoying John, her husband, and Mercy Otis Warren was importuning Thomas Jefferson, her friend, to have "the blessings of liberty to ourselves and our posterity" guaranteed for women as well as men in the Constitution of the United States. In 1844 Margaret Fuller's *Women in the Nineteenth Century*, and her virile pamphlet, "The Great Lawsuit," circulated all over the United States and reminded thousands of women that they had never been satisfied with a condition of legal subjection. The discontent however was an individual affair until 1848, when something new did come into the world, a sense of sex solidarity, a consciousness among women that they had ideals and interests in common, quite apart from what, under one name or another, had always been considered woman's sole existence. This sex solidarity, sex trust and confidence, a thing which men had always known, was to women so novel, so startling, and so enchanting, that the majority might have been content for years merely to meet and talk about it. . . .

A PIONEER IN THE WILDERNESS

A place in the public forum, or even the right of free speech therein, was not enough for Susan B. Anthony. To a mind like hers ideas and action are always inseparable, and to her the newly developed sex solidarity of women was of no value unless it could be put to work to remold the whole of society. Like another pioneer, ax in hand facing the unbroken wilderness, Susan paused only long enough to consider in which direction to blaze the first trail. She was not long in doubt. Returning in September, 1853, from the fourth annual Woman's Rights Convention in Cleveland, where as usual she had been placed on the business and financial committee, she set out on an organization tour through the southern tier of counties in New York. Just a year before she had been over the same territory in the interests of her State Temperance Society, and now she found that practically every lodge she had founded had languished and disappeared. Always for the same reason; the women had no money, no way of getting money, to continue the work. Women, on whom the perpetuation and the nurture of the race depended, were as propertyless as slaves. In a civilization which could not exist without their creative labor they were a pauper class. A sweeping survey of this situation was enough to show Susan where her first trail must lead. In her journal she wrote, with an indignation she hardly knew how to put into words:

> Thus as I passed from town to town I was made to feel the great evil of woman's utter dependence on man for the necessary means to aid reform movements. I never before took in so fully the grand idea of pecuniary independence. Woman must have a purse of her own, and how can this be, so long as the law denies to the wife all right to both the individual and the joint earnings? There is no true freedom for woman without the possession of equal property rights, and these can be obtained only through legislation. If this be so the sooner the demand is made the sooner it will be granted. It must be done by petition, this too at the very next session of the legislature.

Back to Rochester she turned, and by the time the slow and erratic train service got her there she had a complete program, first for a preliminary convention in her home town to draft the petitions and arrange for their circulation, and next for a State Convention at Albany and a descent on the Legislature. Mrs. Stanton must write an address—two addresses—for Susan determined to face the legislators herself, and this Mrs. Stanton agreed to do, although her many domestic cares, she feared, would probably make it impossible for her to attend the Rochester meeting. Susan must furnish the material for the speeches. Susan usually did.

"Can you not get an acute lawyer—," wrote Mrs. Stanton, "perhaps Judge Hay is the man—sufficiently interested in our movement to look up just eight laws concerning us—the very worst in all the code? I can generalize and philosophize easily enough by myself but the details of the laws I have not time to look up. . . . While I am about the house, surrounded by my children, washing dishes, sewing, baking, etc., I can think up many points, but I cannot search books. . . . Men who can, when they wish to write a document, shut themselves up for days with their thoughts and their books, know little of what difficulties a woman must surmount to get off a tolerable production."

Judge William Hay, of Saratoga, to whom Susan wrote post haste, consented to look up the eight worst laws, but apparently when he got into the code he could not make up his mind which of all the bad ones were the worst, so he sent Susan thirteen. . . . The radical Quakers and the Rev. Mr. William Henry Channing gladly agreed to help Susan with her Rochester convention, but it was her hand that penned most of the letters, scores of letters, to influential people throughout the State, asking for their signatures; to editors begging for publicity; to men and women inviting them to come to Rochester and help circulate the petitions. Susan hired a hall, arranged for ushers, speakers, advertising, lights, all the troublesome minutiæ. The convention unanimously elected her chairman of the committee on petitions, and immediately after the meeting she selected sixty women as captains, and dividing the State into districts she assigned each woman her place. Susan and her captains then went out into the cold and storm of a New York winter in a house to house canvass for names. Like itinerant tin pedlars or book agents they tramped the streets and country roads, knocking at every door, presenting their petitions, arguing with women who half the time slammed the door in their faces with the smug remark that *they* had husbands, thank God, to look after their interests, and they needed no new laws to protect their rights. After each rebuff the women simply trudged on to the next street, the next row of houses, the next grudgingly opened front doors. In ten weeks' time they secured 6,000 signatures to the petition asking for laws granting married women the right to collect and control their own earnings, and the right of equal guardianship of their children. Surprisingly they secured on the petition for equal suffrage 4,000 names.

PETITIONING THE LEGISLATORS

The State Convention met in Albany, February 14, 1854, with Mrs. Stanton presiding, and Susan very busy in the background, seeing that Mrs. Stanton's splendid address was printed in time to have a copy on each legislator's desk on the opening day of the convention, and 50,000 copies printed and mailed to every corner of the State. The two bills were introduced and were referred to a joint committee of the Senate and Assembly, and these gentlemen Susan was, as a great favor, permitted to address. . . . With her clear contralto voice, her perfect enunciation, her fine economy of words, she could not fail to impress on the men the earnestness of her errand. Yet they must have been sorely puzzled, those politicians, to hear solemnly recited a long catalogue of laws which they had always taken for granted as right and proper, and to be told that she, Susan B. Anthony, and all her colleagues proposed to come before the Legislature every year, as long as they lived, until these laws were erased from the books. Married women must have all the rights of single women, exactly as though the husbands did not exist. They must own and control their property, their wages; they must be allowed to will and devise their property like men; they must be allowed freely to contract, to sue and be sued; they must be equal guardians of their minor children, and while joint property laws should be enacted, women should be subject to proportional liability for the support of children; homesteads must be made inviolable and inalienable for widows and children; habitual drunkenness must be made cause for divorce; and finally, in order that they might aid in the securing of equal laws, women married and unmarried, must be given the right to vote. They must be eligible to all offices, occupations, professions, be entitled to serve on juries, and to be employed in public offices. The whole code must be revised, extending the masculine designation to women. One committeeman went on record as saying that it gave him gooseflesh to hear an unmarried female advocate such destructive changes in the protected status of loved and cherished wives.

More of the assembled legislators must have experienced cold chills when they listened to the longer and more passionate speech of Elizabeth Cady Stanton, for although the chairman of the joint committee, James L. Angle of Monroe County, recommended a bill allowing married women to collect and control their own earnings, whenever their husbands were proven dissolute or neglectful, and providing that children of tender years might not be apprenticed to trades without the written consent of their mothers, House and Senate alike, by a very large majority, voted adversely. The speeches of the opposition were in essence identical.

"Are we, sir," demanded Mr. Burnett of Essex, addressing the speaker of the Assembly against the bill granting married women their right to wages and the guardianship of children, "to give the least countenance to claims so preposterous, disgraceful and criminal as are embodied in this address? Are we to put the stamp of truth upon the libel here set forth that men and women in the matrimonial relation are to be equal? We *know* that God created man as the representative of the race; that after his creation the Creator took from his side the material for woman's creation; and that by the institution of matrimony, woman was restored to the side of man, and that they became one flesh and one being, he being the head. . . ." If such a felicitous arrangement were ever interfered with by law makers, said the speaker, there would be no way of preserving men's honor except by locking wives behind bolts and bars, "as in Italy."

From the galleries the women delegates listened with sick hearts, but the iron-nerved Susan heard it all without even a sign of impatience. She knew that neither Mr. Burnett of Essex nor any of his colleagues really believed such nonsense. They were simply uttering inherited opinions, very conveniently brought forth and aired for their own defense. If some did believe it, very well, they must be made to change their minds. Before a larger and more insistent public opinion they would have to change. Therefore, to work again, collecting more petitions, more and more names, until the Legislature was swamped with them. "Napoleon," Mr. Channing now christened her. . . .

ALL ON HER OWN

The Saratoga incident that summer was typical. Susan heard that a large temperance convention was to be held in Saratoga, and simultaneously an Anti-Nebraska meeting [opposing the 1854 Kansas-Nebraska Act, which repealed the provision of the Missouri Compromise that restricted the expansion of slavery in the western territories], and to that renowned summer resort she immediately repaired to hold a woman's rights meeting the same week. She dispatched hasty letters to Mrs. Stanton, Mrs. Lucretia Mott, Lucy Stone, and Rev. Antoinette Brown and the ardent Ernestine Rose, every good speaker she knew, urging the great advantage of holding meetings, and of circulating petitions in such audiences as they should certainly draw from the two other conventions. Confident that some of the women at least would respond, Susan went on with her arrangements, with great difficulty renting a hall and advertising her meeting. But when the morning of the day arrived not a single one of the faithful was on hand. Each woman was preoccupied with her domestic or professional duties, each relied on the others to go, and of course nobody turned up. So here was Susan, in debt for a hall, for handbills and newspaper notices, without a speaker or even a presiding officer. To add to her troubles she had had her pocket book lifted by some adroit thief, and the money, fifteen dollars, happened to be every penny she possessed. However, she said nothing about that to her friend Judge Hay, to whom in despair she now turned. The Judge was no speaker, but he encouraged Susan to get out and polish up that speech Mrs. Stanton had written for her a year ago, and together they scoured the town for a possible chairman. To their joy they found at one of the huge hotels two woman's rights adherents, Matilda Joslyn Gage and Sarah Pellet, a recent graduate of Oberlin, the first coeducational college. Both consented to speak, and Susan, in addition to presiding, gave her speech, by this time enriched with pungent interpolations of her own. Twenty-five cents admission was charged, but even so the hall was not large enough to hold the curious crowd. . . . The meeting was a wonderful success, many names went on the petition and so many tracts were sold that, what with admissions and all, Susan had money to pay her expenses, give ten dollars apiece to her speakers, and forgetful of the stolen fifteen dollars go home in comfort. And that took money, in 1854, for the journey from Saratoga to Albany alone involved eight hours in jolting railroad trains, with several changes of cars and much waiting on hard benches between trains. . . .

Seven months of this sort of thing in one year might have discouraged some, but to Susan the campaign of 1854 was but an appetizer of what was to come in the two years following. She now conceived the idea, which after a national convention in Philadelphia, in October, became a stern purpose, of canvassing every county in New York State with petitions to be rained down on the next legislature. No woman had ever done such a thing. . . .

With her father as security she went into debt for a few thousand handbills advertising her lectures. . . . Having spent every dollar of her surplus Susan wrote to Wendell Phillips who had taken a prominent part in the Philadelphia convention, asking him if there had been any money left over. He replied that the funds were quite exhausted, but he enclosed a personal check for fifty dollars, a loan, he said, although he never did allow Susan to pay it back. With this fifty dollars in hand, not a penny besides, Susan left home on Christmas day, 1854, with a head full of plans, a heart full of courage, and a carpet bag full of campaign literature and petitions for the legislature. Her mother and sister wept to see her go, and even Daniel held his daughter fast in his arms for a moment before he could bring himself to let her board the shabby train out of Rochester. The winter was the coldest and snowiest known in ten years, the wooden cars were furnished with wood stoves which alternated between being red hot and stone cold, and in whatever town tavern or country farm house she would be sleeping for the next months her hardships would be great. But at least her father left her free to go wherever conviction led her, and that far Susan was better off than most women of her generation.

The adventures of that winter deserve much more space than can possibly be given them here. In some towns she had fine meetings, enthusiastic audiences, and no end of "York shillings" in the collection box. In others not a church or schoolhouse could be obtained, and at one town, Olean, the meeting would have had to be abandoned had not the landlord of the hotel offered his dining-room. At Angelica, nine towns represented, as the diary records, crowded houses. A young minister signs his name to the petition, but hastily scratches it off when one of his rich parishioners threatens to leave the church unless the name is withdrawn. At Mayville, Chautauqua County, she has to spend fifty-six cents for four pounds of candles to light the hall. . . .

ENDURANCE AND DETERMINATION

In February, 1855, Susan broke off long enough to visit the Legislature with hugely augmented petitions, but she could get no new bills introduced that session, so off again, this time into the icy fastnesses of the Lake George and Schroon Lake districts. Nowhere in the State were all towns connected by railroads, and in this isolated region Susan had to depend almost entirely on stage-coaches. She finds it almost too much to endure at times, she confesses, but once in a while a little relief arrives. A gentleman who had been an interested auditor in Albany turns up mysteriously just as she is about to take the stage for Lake George. He has a thick plank baked delightfully hot, and begs permission to place it under her feet. As often as the stage halts he dashes out and has the plank reheated, and with his own hands brings her cups of steaming tea. A day or two later the same handsome, bearded stranger turns up again, this time with a fine sleigh and a pair of spanking gray horses, and drives her to his sister's home for an over-Sunday rest. From town to town he insists on driving Susan, buried in fur robes and her feet deliciously warm on the hot plank. Several days of her unusual conversation, the proximity of her vital body, and the gentleman's heart suddenly overflows, and he totally ruins the situation by bursting forth and imploring Susan to leave this terrible life and share his heart, his home and his hot plank forever. Susan cannot make him understand that this terrible life is the only one she finds endurable, and so he turns back, swearing by heaven that these modern women are too much for the ordinary man's comprehension. Stage-coaches seem pretty uncomfortable for a while after that. The snowdrifts are over the fences in many places and roads are so badly blocked that vehicles have to take to the ice-covered meadows. Susan's feet, frost bitten no doubt, begin to give her serious trouble. She soaks them in cold water, then wraps them in woolens, but the pain merely transfers itself to her back. All the way to Malone she has to sit doubled over, clinging to the seat in front in order not to groan aloud. She holds her meeting in spite of suffering, gets to Ogdensburg, then to Canton. But when the time arrives to leave this point she has to be carried to the stage. Ten miles from Watertown she changes to the train, barely able to walk, and arriving at the hotel in late afternoon she determines to give the "water cure," sovereign remedy of the age, a final test. She sends for a chambermaid, orders two buckets of ice water, and sitting in a coffin-like tin tub, has both buckets poured over her aching body. Wrapped in hot blankets she sleeps through the night and, believe it or not, wakes up in the morning as good as new.

The first of May Susan reached home, exhausted but triumphant. In four months she had lectured and circulated petitions in fifty-four of the sixty counties of the State, collected $2,367, expended $2,291, and has a balance left over of $76. For herself? What a question! For the first expenses of the campaign of 1856.

Anthony's Unheeded Warnings: The Setback of the Civil War

Bill Severn

With the onset of the Civil War, most supporters of women's rights felt that they should curtail their activities for the duration of the conflict. They feared that continuing to engage in political agitation for women's suffrage during a time of warfare would be seen as unpatriotic and would hinder their cause. They also hoped that by supporting the Union's war effort, they would prove to the government and the general populace that women were worthy of the right to vote. As Bill Severn points out, Susan B. Anthony was the only prominent leader who disagreed with this assessment: She warned that they risked losing the movement's momentum and the few gains they had already achieved. In the following excerpt from his book *Free but Not Equal: How Women Won the Right to Vote*, Severn describes the fulfillment of Anthony's misgivings after the war, as Congress passed amendments that specifically excluded women from the right to vote.

Susan Anthony tried to keep alive the battle for woman's rights as the growing threat of Civil War gripped the nation. War talk or not, she felt it was no time to abandon the crusade or all the gains of the years before would be lost. But she couldn't get much support for her call for another national suffrage convention after the one that was held in Albany, New York, in 1861. Her abolitionist friends argued that the question of woman's rights would have to be put aside until freedom was won for the Negro.

"All our reformers seem suddenly to have grown politic," she wrote a friend. "All alike say, 'Have no conventions at this crisis . . . wait until the war excitement abates.' I am sick at heart, but cannot carry the world against the wish and will of our best friends."

Unable to arouse any interest in woman's rights, she and Elizabeth Stanton joined other leaders of the woman's movement in the fight for Negro freedom. As a Quaker, Susan abhored the very thought of war, but as she put it, "I cannot feel easy in my conscience to be dumb in an hour like this."

FACING HOSTILE CROWDS

It was a time when many people in the North still favored compromise with the slave states to hold the nation together. Abolitionists were looked upon as dangerous radicals for their stand that it was better to let the South secede, even at the risk of splitting the Union apart, than to fasten slavery more firmly upon the Negro. Susan and Elizabeth began a lecture tour of New York state to denounce any compromise with slavery.

Mobs turned against them in every city where they spoke. A crowd of men brandishing knives and pistols invaded the hall in Syracuse. An audience in Buffalo hissed, yelled and stamped up such a racket the speakers couldn't be heard. Their banners proclaiming "No Union with Slaveholders" were ripped down. At another meeting the mob put out the lights and threatened to pull Susan from the platform. She stood her ground in the dark until lanterns were brought and she went on speaking. In Rochester police had to rescue her and Elizabeth and escort them home through a threatening crowd.

In some places the police refused to come to their defense and they were roughly pushed around and pelted with ripe vegetables and rotten eggs. Mobs took over the platforms and sang and hooted. Crowds dragged effigies of them through the streets and burned them in public squares. Mayor George Hornell Thacher of Albany, who insisted on their right of free speech in that city, personally escorted them to the hall and sat with a loaded pistol on his lap to enforce order. But he asked them to call off another meeting that was planned and they had to agree. The unruly mobs finally convinced them they had little chance of getting their message across and Susan and Elizabeth brought their speaking tour to an end.

When civil war finally came, the faction of the Republican Party known as the Radicals soon rose to power in Washington. Among them were the leading abolitionists. They were the friends Susan Anthony was counting on to help win the vote for women when the war ended. She was determined to rally the nation's women behind them in the fight to win approval for the 13th Amendment to forever ban Negro slavery.

Elizabeth Stanton and her husband had moved to New York City. Susan joined her there and they drew up a call for a meeting of "The Loyal Women of the Nation" to be held in New York on May 14, 1863. They sent it to all the women they knew from their earlier campaigns for woman's rights. The summons to "counsel with one another" over the problems of self-government in which "woman is equally interested and responsible with man" brought hundreds of women to New York. Susan, Elizabeth and Lucy Stone addressed the gathering and Angelina Grimké came out of retirement to urge support for the 13th Amendment.

Susan got the group to pledge that they would collect thousands of signatures to a petition asking Congress to pass the anti-slavery amendment. They organized the Woman's Loyal League, with Elizabeth as president and Susan as secretary, opened a small office and got their project underway. For the next fifteen months they worked to get signatures, with the aid of other women all across the country to California. Men also joined in the campaign until there was a volunteer force of some two thousand circulating petitions. Hundreds of children helped sort, count and wrap them. By the time the drive was finished they had collected almost 400,000 signatures, a total big enough to impress even some of the most reluctant congressmen.

Symbolic of the slaves the amendment sought to free, two tall Negroes carried the huge rolls of petitions from all the northern states into the chamber of the United States Senate and placed them on the desk of Senator Charles Sumner of Massachusetts, the Senate's Radical leader and sponsor of the amendment. "This petition marks a stage of public opinion in the history of slavery," Sumner told the Senate. "Though memorable for their numbers, these petitioners are more memorable still for the prayer in which they unite. They ask nothing less than universal emancipation; and this they ask directly at the hands of Congress."

The petitions, of course, didn't bring about passage of the

13th Amendment, but the work the women did played no small part in influencing that decision. Although they had no vote they had taken an active part in national politics. By working together over the months in every state of the Union they gained experience and understanding of the value of organized effort to get what they wanted.

War itself brought thousands of women into new activities that strengthened their independence and proved they could do physically hard work under rough and dangerous conditions. Women nursed the war wounded, maintained hospitals and hospital ships, relief camps and convalescent homes. They provided bandages, medicine, food for the troops, and served in more dramatic ways. Many women left at home by men who had gone to war were forced to take over the full management of family affairs. They had to do men's tasks to house, clothe and feed their families.

Women were needed in shops and factories, in all sorts of jobs once done only by men. New teaching positions were opened to them, government offices, opportunities that brought them out of their homes to work, speak, and even to campaign politically at the side of men. The lives they led during the war helped, more than years of arguing for their rights, to disprove the old idea that woman's place was only in the home.

When peace came, the hopes of the suffragists ran high. They believed that a nation grateful to its women for all they had done in the war would willingly reward them with the right to vote. Growing numbers of men had come to agree that women should have that right. The Republican Radicals, whom the women had strongly supported when the fight against slavery was unpopular, held almost dictatorial power in Congress. Sweeping changes in the Constitution were planned to write into the nation's laws the decisions that had been made on the field of battle.

The Negro was to be guaranteed the right to vote and the women felt the time had never been better to gain that right for themselves than when the basic law of the land was being rewritten by the political leaders they considered their friends. Susan Anthony declared there must be full citizenship for the woman as well as for the Negro. She warned that if they delayed, if they let the issue be put aside, it might be years before such an opportunity came again.

She was stunned when her old friend Wendell Phillips

told her the two movements should not be joined. The cause of woman's rights always had been fought from the same platforms as the fight against slavery, but Phillips wrote her in May 1865 that while he hadn't changed his mind about suffrage for women, "I would not mix the movements." He said demands by the women might risk loss of citizenship for the Negro. "I think such a mixture would lose for the Negro much more than we should gain for the woman," he wrote.

In a rather curt reply Susan asked, "Do you believe the African race is composed entirely of males?"

But she was dismayed to learn that most of the other abolitionists felt as he did. "This is the Negro's hour," she was told. "The woman's hour will come." They argued that slavery had been a stormy national issue for thirty-five years, war had been fought over it, and the North was emotionally ready to see justice done for the Negro, but nobody was that

---

Our Gains Are Snatched from Us

In one of their major tactical disagreements, Susan B. Anthony and Elizabeth Cady Stanton differed over the suspension of the women's rights movement during the Civil War, as Elizabeth Frost and Kathryn Cullen-DuPont explain in the following excerpt from Women's Suffrage in America: An Eyewitness History. *According to the authors, the movement began losing ground almost immediately with the reversal of key portions of New York's Married Woman's Property Act—a piece of legislation that had taken Anthony years of hard work to get passed.*

When the Civil War began in the spring of 1861, Elizabeth Cady Stanton and Susan B. Anthony had to make a decision: How should members of the women's movement respond? Elizabeth Cady Stanton thought that their activities should be discontinued during the war. She viewed this as a tactical move. It was a detour—but also a chance for women to prove their worth as citizens. The war "to preserve the Union" would become, she thought, a war to end slavery. The women's rights activists, many of whom had strong abolitionist backgrounds, would involve themselves in the Union cause, and contributions as citizens would make it clear that they were entitled to the vote. Cady Stanton was sure of this.

Susan B. Anthony disagreed. If women, for whatever reason, stopped pressing their claim, their claim would be ignored. Women would get the vote, Anthony believed, only if they con-

concerned over woman's rights. It was a side issue, she was told, one that would only arouse controversy. The abolitionists asked her to be patient. "It is a matter of method," Phillips wrote, "of expedient action."

Politicians urged her to be practical. With enough support they might make suffrage for male Negroes part of the Constitution in a 14th Amendment, but their efforts could fail if the women interfered. Senator Sumner, who had praised women so highly for their petition work against slavery, thought any move to include them in the planned amendment would be "ill-advised." On the other side of Congress, Thaddeus Stevens, the Radical leader of the House, who always before had been friendly to the woman's movement, was equally determined not to let them get in the way of his party's program. Women would not be overlooked, he promised, when their time came, but it wasn't now.

tinued to demand it. It would not be granted as a reward for patriotism, valor or sacrifice. Susan B. Anthony was equally sure of her position.

Virtually all of the women's rights leaders shared Cady Stanton's viewpoint. Finally, when not one prominent woman aligned herself with Anthony, she acquiesced. The Albany women's rights convention of February 1861 would be the last for a while. Until the war ended, Anthony would put aside women's rights work as such and urge others to do the same. . . .

And yet, something less than rewarding happened: In 1862, as American women were becoming widowed in unprecedented numbers, the New York State legislature replaced key portions of the state's Married Woman's Property Act of 1860. A mother's hard-won right to equal custody of her children and her right to use a deceased husband's estate for the benefit of her children were abolished. "Well, well," Anthony wrote to her friend Lydia Mott, "while the old guard sleep the young 'devils' are wide-awake, and we deserve to suffer for our confidence in 'man's sense of justice,' and to have all we have gained thus snatched from us."

It was only the first sign that Susan B. Anthony might have been right.

Elizabeth Frost and Kathryn Cullen-DuPont, *Women's Suffrage in America: An Eyewitness History*, 1992.

FRANTIC EFFORTS

Susan was visiting a brother in Kansas when Elizabeth Stanton sent her the alarming news that the Radical leaders, instead of favoring women, intended to write the word "male" into the 14th Amendment in a way that would raise the question as to whether women were even legal citizens of the United States. "Come back and help," Elizabeth pleaded. "There is pressing need."

While Susan was hurrying back East, Elizabeth and the others used all their influence to try to keep the proposed amendment from including the word "male" to define a citizen. Lucy Stone personally went to Washington and begged Senator Sumner to change it. He told her he had tried, but he saw no way around it. "I sat up all one night and rewrote that clause of the amendment fourteen times, so unwilling was I to introduce the word 'male' into the Constitution," he said, "but I could find no other way to embody my meaning."

The women's protest was no mere feminine whim against the use of the masculine word. In various states women had been barred from voting by laws that classified them with children, idiots and criminals and restricted voting citizenship solely to adult males. But that definition of citizenship had never before been part of the basic federal law. The planned new amendment would make women inferior to the male Negroes they had helped free from slavery. They feared it might mean that even if they won the right to vote in individual states they would be barred from voting in federal elections and would be faced with the seemingly impossible task of putting through another amendment to change the Constitution again.

"As our Constitution now exists, there is nothing to prevent women or Negroes from holding the ballot but state legislation," Elizabeth wrote. "But if that word 'male' is inserted as now proposed it will take us a century at least to get it out again."

When Susan arrived in New York she and Elizabeth went to work to try to revive the suffrage movement that had been almost inactive since the start of the Civil War. Many former leaders had lost interest and were busy with other things, with new jobs or professions, and with the vast changes war had brought their homes and families. Five years had passed since the last national convention. Suffrage workers were scattered and some didn't even bother to answer letters sent to them. Others agreed with the abolitionists who thought it was the wrong time to fight for woman's rights.

Susan made a trip to New England to line up the support of prominent people she knew there. She tried to get the famous author Ralph Waldo Emerson to declare himself in favor of an immediate appeal to Congress. "Ask my wife," Emerson told her. "I can philosophize but I always look to her to decide for me in practical matters." Susan did just that and won Mrs. Emerson's backing for a campaign to petition Congress. When she returned to New York she carried with her the public endorsements of a number of other well-known New Englanders whose names were sure to get attention from the newspapers.

She and Elizabeth drew up petitions and sent them to women who previously had been active in the movement. They asked them to sign a plea to both houses of Congress for "an amendment to the Constitution that shall prohibit the several states from disfranchising any of their citizens on the ground of sex." It was the first time in history that suffragists had made a direct request to Congress for action to grant them the vote. They presented the Congress of 1866 with petitions bearing ten thousand signatures. But nothing was done. Sumner reluctantly presented one of the petitions in the Senate, but only after protesting that he considered the whole thing "most inopportune."

Woman suffrage was debated in Congress for the first time several months later. It came up in connection with a move to extend the vote to Negroes in the District of Columbia. But the majority stood firmly against striking the word "male" out of the District bill. Representative Richard Williams of Oregon warned that if women ever were able to get into politics they would "convert all the now harmonious elements of society into a state of war and make every home a hell on earth."

DISSENSION IN THE MOVEMENT

The first woman's-rights convention since the war finally was called to meet in New York in May, 1866. Its leaders were sharply divided over what women should do about the proposed 14th Amendment. The arguments put Susan and Elizabeth and their old friend Lucy Stone on opposite sides. Lucy agreed that the wording should be changed, but felt that if it couldn't be changed women should still give the amendment their full support. She warned against making any voting demands of their own that might endanger the amendment and said it was vital for Negroes to get their rights even if women had to wait.

"I will be thankful in my soul," Lucy said, "if *anybody* can get out of the terrible pit."

There was no disloyalty to Negroes, Susan answered, in demanding that all of them should have the right to vote and not just the half who were male. Whatever their color, she insisted, the rights of all women should not be sacrificed to men. She had fought against slavery, risked personal danger to crusade for Negro freedom, but she also wanted woman's freedom from continued political slavery.

"I will cut off this right arm of mine," she declared, "before I will ever work for or demand the ballot for the Negro and not the woman."

A compromise was reached and the convention resolved itself into the American Equal Rights Association, to work for suffrage for both women and Negroes, with Lucretia Mott as its president, but the split between the two factions was not healed. It was a parting of the ways that would widen as the abolitionists gained control of the new association and turned it away from seeking woman's rights. Susan and Lucy had shared the battles for suffrage, but they soon found themselves leading opposite camps.

When the 14th Amendment was passed by Congress in June, 1866, and sent to the states for ratification with the limiting word "male" still in it, Susan and her group felt the nation's women had been "sold out" by the politicians who had always called themselves their friends. She and Elizabeth vowed to carry on the fight by taking it into the states that would have to ratify the amendment. They still hoped to keep the states from making it part of the Constitution.

A LOSING BATTLE

Susan Anthony and Elizabeth Stanton began their battle against the "male only" 14th Amendment in their own state of New York by presenting petitions to the legislature. But it was a losing battle from the start, there and in other states, and it cost them the support of many former followers. . . .

Another blow to woman suffrage came in July 1868 when the states finally ratified the "male only" 14th Amendment. On top of it, the Radical leaders in Congress moved to put through a 15th Amendment, which again left out the women. Susan promptly demanded a new amendment that would clearly guarantee woman's constitutional right to vote. Lucy Stone and her followers argued that the demand was not realistic, that women couldn't hope for federal action until they won themselves national political strength by first gaining voting rights in the various states.

Susan issued a call for a convention to meet in New York that would be devoted solely to woman suffrage, and in May 1869 the American Equal Rights Association finally broke apart. Susan and Elizabeth worked swiftly to organize the National Woman Suffrage Association, with a membership open only to women. Lucy Stone and her followers formed a second organization several months later in Cleveland. Called the American Woman Suffrage Association, it included men among its leaders as well as representatives of some of the established state suffrage groups.

Despite many attempts on both sides to bring them back together, the two suffrage organizations went their independent ways for the next twenty years. Susan and the National Association carried on an unending fight for an amendment to the Constitution while Lucy and the American Association worked more in the individual states. Their efforts often overlapped, both in Washington and in state campaigns, but Lucy's group was more conservative in its methods and policies than Susan's.

Susan and the National Association took sides on all the issues involving woman's rights. With a liberal outlook and crusading spirit they freely voiced their opinions on questions of politics, divorce, the attitude of the churches, and the organization of women into labor unions. Lucy and the American Association tried to avoid discussing anything but woman's right to vote. She believed that raising other issues might cost the support of male voters and politicians. Both associations worked hard for woman suffrage, but in different ways.

Anthony's *Revolution:* The First Feminist Newspaper

Lynne Masel-Walters

In 1868, Susan B. Anthony became the cofounder and proprietor of a weekly newspaper, the *Revolution*, which was the first national periodical devoted to the cause of women's rights. Anthony only managed to publish the *Revolution* for two years; the newspaper's content was too radical for many readers, and despite her best efforts, she was unable to keep it afloat financially. Yet during its brief life, the *Revolution* had a major impact on the women's rights movement, opening up new and daring topics for discussion. Lynne Masel-Walters, a professor of journalism at Texas A&M University in College Station, explores the history and the legacy of the *Revolution* in the following article.

> Men, their rights and nothing more;
> Women, their rights and nothing less.

Such was the goal of suffragists Elizabeth Cady Stanton and Susan B. Anthony and of *The Revolution,* the newspaper they published from 1868–1870. Though a just aim, it was distant because, in the 19th century, women had few rights, least of all the right to vote. But neither the suffragists nor their publication lived to see their goal realized. Despite this failure, *The Revolution* had an important place in the history of suffrage journalism and the feminist struggle. The first major national publication concerned with feminine equality, *The Revolution* championed not only voting rights but women's rights in general. It was also the most loyal to the cause. During the "Negro's hour," when the woman's struggle was forgotten or postponed, *The Revolution* continued fighting

From "Their Rights and Nothing More: A History of *The Revolution*, 1868–70," by Lynne Masel-Walters, *Journalism Quarterly,* Summer 1976. Reprinted with permission.

for the female. But the fight it prompted was not just external. *The Revolution* also served as a catalyst for a split that affected the suffrage movement for 30 years. But what was *The Revolution?* Who were the personalities that shaped it? How did it relate to contemporary events? What issues filled its pages? And what was its impact?

A WORLD OF RAPID CHANGES

The Revolution was a child of turbulent times, for the years 1868 to 1870 were filled with disturbing changes in American life. The Civil War was over, but its wounds were not healed. Intra-party political warfare between conservative and radical Republicans was bitter; the few surviving Democrats were hardly a factor. The revered Lincoln was dead, his successor facing impeachment. And, although legally emancipated, the former slave was not yet free.

Elsewhere other profound changes were occurring. The American city was beginning to emerge. Built by immigrants from foreign lands and domestic farms, the city wrought an upheaval disturbing to believers in the ideal of the yeoman farmer. These dissidents formed splinter political parties to protect their interests against those of the growing urban centers.

Different in form and number than earlier cities, the urban center was both the mother and child of other dislocations in American society. The foreigner and the factory provided increased workers and work places. Thus, business boomed. Greed led to savage business and industrial competition and to the rise of monopolistic combines. Too much was happening too fast and it was difficult for Americans to keep hold of the turbulent, changing world.

The woman suffrage movement in 1868 was in nearly as much disarray as the country. Before the Civil War, women had almost succeeded in winning the vote. But sectional strife brought an abrupt end to suffrage agitation as feminists joined the war effort. They formed a Woman's Loyalty League and collected 400,000 signatures on a petition calling for immediate emancipation of the slave. The League also conducted a propaganda campaign that convinced many Northerners the war was a crusade to regenerate society.

This propaganda worked against women, for, when the war was over, Americans snubbed female rights and focused attention on black equality. This was true of the former champions of woman suffrage. Horace Greeley, Gerrit Smith, Wendell Phillips and others told women to stand aside. Republicans, Abolitionists, and even some women believed that this was the "Negro's hour." Black enfranchisement was a party measure, a political necessity and the culmination of the anti-slavery struggle. Knowing this, imbued with the politicians' idea of one reform at a time, and trained in self-sacrifice, most women gave up their claim to enfranchisement.

Not all women did. Elizabeth Cady Stanton and Susan B. Anthony, founders and leaders of the woman's rights movement, remained stalwart, campaigning throughout the country for the woman's vote. One of those campaigns was in Kansas. That state, in 1868, was holding a double referendum. One resolution proposed to remove the word "white" from the voters' qualifications; the other to remove the word "male." Stanton and Anthony stumped that state for the passage of the latter referendum.

Their resolution lost, but the Kansas campaign brought the two women together with George Francis Train. A Copperhead [a Southern sympathizer], an eccentric, a millionaire financier, a proponent of the Fenian [Irish] Revolution, Turkish baths and the water cure, Train lately had become interested in the woman's cause. Enthusiastically, he joined the Kansas campaign of Stanton and Anthony. Train's fancy clothes and oratory charmed his audiences. His desire to help the female's cause, when nobody else would, charmed the two suffrage leaders.

Their affection for Train grew when, near the end of the Kansas tour, he offered Anthony money to start a woman suffrage newspaper. Speaking one night in Junction City, Train announced:

> When Miss Anthony gets back to New York, she is going to start a suffrage paper. Its name is to be *The Revolution;* its motto "Men, their rights and nothing more; women, their rights and nothing less." Let everybody subscribe for it!

Train's offer thrilled Stanton and Anthony. For years they had wanted to start a suffrage newspaper but had never found the money. The Equal Rights Association often had talked of raising funds for such an organ, but never translated its words into action. The Hovey Fund, established to further universal suffrage, also was asked to finance a woman's publication. However, the Fund was deeply committed to the black cause, directing all its money to the *Antislavery Standard.* This irritated the woman suffragists, since slavery had already been abolished. Complained Stanton, " . . . for the noble women who have labored 34 years to lift the black man to their own level, there is broader work to-day than to exhalt him *above* their own heads."

To accomplish this "broader work," Stanton and Anthony accepted Train's offer despite his eccentric background. The women returned to New York and began *The Revolution,* joined in their endeavor by Parker Pillsbury. Like Stanton, Pillsbury was a prolific and courageous writer. He was a good friend of the suffragists. An experienced journalist and reformer, Pillsbury had worked on the *Antislavery Standard.* But, thinking the journal was doing too little for woman suffrage, Pillsbury left the *Standard* and gladly joined the staff of *The Revolution.*

Aided by other stalwart suffragists, Stanton, Anthony and Pillsbury published the first weekly issue of *The Revolution* on Jan. 8, 1868. The 10,000 copies of the 16-page newspaper were sent throughout the country under the frank of James Brooks, Democratic congressman from New York. Announcing itself the organ of the National Party of New America, *The Revolution* said it was devoted to principle, not policy; suffrage, irrespective of color or sex; equal pay for equal work; the eight-hour day; abolition of party despotism; the regeneration of American society; and "Down with politicians, up with people.". . .

The first issue of *The Revolution* received mixed reviews. The *Daily Times* of Troy (New York) said the woman's paper was "readable, well-edited and instructive." Although *The Revolution's* ideas were impracticable, the *Daily Times* continued, "its beautiful mechanical execution renders the appearance very attractive." The Cambridge, (Massachusetts) *Press* called *The Revolution* a "great fact," while the Chicago *Times* praised the publication as a "readable sheet, well printed and well written, bold and independent." The Providence, (Rhode Island) *Press* said that the editors of *The Revolution* "have an irrepressible spirit, and if they do not produce a revolution it will be the first time that justice and freedom persistently set forth fail of accomplishing a grand result."

Other newspapers were less laudatory. The New York *Times* said that *The Revolution* was a victim of illogical thinking and that its motto was "meaningless and foolish." The New York Sunday *Atlas* and the Rochester (New York) *Evening* complained that the woman's publication "smacks very strongly of Train." The New York *World* gave the newspaper and its proprietress a backhanded compliment:

> If she [Anthony] were a confiding miss of 'sweet sixteen' instead of the strong-minded woman that she is, . . . we suspect (such is the infirmity or perversity of 'those odious men') that she would make more conquests than she can reasonably expect to do with the intellectual blaze and brilliancy of this week's *Revolution. . . .*

Horace Greeley's New York *Tribune* and Wendell Phillips' *Antislavery Standard* did more than criticize *The Revolution;* they ignored it. The latter would not even accept a paid advertisement of the paper. Since the men and their newspapers previously had been friends of the woman's movement, this silence deeply distressed Stanton and Anthony. . . .

The treatment of *The Revolution* by Greeley and Phillips was indicative of more conservative suffragists' reaction to the publication and its sponsors. There were many reasons for this hostility. The newspaper's name was too inflammatory. The association with Democrats and Copperheads was deplorable. And the affiliation with Train, a Negrophobe, was unpardonable. In a letter to Anthony, William Lloyd Garrison said that she and Stanton had "taken leave of good sense" to join with that "crack-brained harlequin and semi-lunatic, George Francis Train." Lucy Stone, the Boston suffrage leader, also was infuriated by the Stanton-Anthony acceptance of Train. "Susan Anthony can be scarcely less crazy than he is," she exploded.

Anthony did not let her financial "angel" go undefended. While admitting that Train had some extravagances and ideosyncracies, she noted that he was willing to devote time and money to the woman's cause when no other man was. "It seems to me," she said, "it would be right and wise to accept aid from the devil himself, provided that he did not tempt us to lower our standard."

The quarrel between Stanton and Anthony and the more conservative suffragists climaxed at the 1869 Equal Rights Association Convention. There, Frederick Douglass, a leading Negro exponent of enfranchisement for his race, successfully lobbied for a resolution supporting the 15th amendment to the United States Constitution. This put the woman's movement in the position of backing a suffrage amendment excluding their sex. It was too much for Stanton and Anthony. They summoned a group of women to the offices of *The Revolution* where they formed the National Woman Suffrage Association (NWSA). Although this group

---

THE *REVOLUTION*'S APPROACH TO WORKING WOMEN

Bonnie J. Dow is a professor of speech communication and women's studies at the University of Georgia in Athens. Her books include Wise Women: Political Cartoons of the Woman Suffrage Movement *and* Prime-Time Feminism: Television, Media Culture, and the Women's Movement Since 1970. *In the following paragraphs, she describes Susan B. Anthony's decision to use the* Revolution *to reach out to working-class women in hopes of converting them to the cause.*

Despite its short life, scholars have agreed that the *Revolution* had a significant impact on the woman's rights movement in the nineteenth century. In one respect, the *Revolution* was important because it gave the woman's rights movement a "forum, focus, and direction," as historian Eleanor Flexner argues; however, the nature of that focus and direction was even more important.

In addition to its discussion of controversial issues in relation to woman suffrage, the *Revolution* also departed from the general tradition of women's journals because it targeted lower-class women laborers as potential beneficiaries of and participants in woman suffrage reforms. From its beginnings, the woman's rights movement had focused on middle- and upper-class women, primarily because such women had the time, resources, and education to pursue reform. Through the *Revolution*, Elizabeth Cady Stanton and Susan B. Anthony attempted to create recognition of the equal stake of working women in equal rights and suffrage. . . .

Anthony's concern for the plight of the working woman eventually resulted in redefinition and expansion of the potential membership of the suffrage movement. . . . Anthony recognized that the working woman's role in the movement had largely been ignored, and she set out to cultivate these women through the *Revolution*. Her goal was clear: to convince working women that the solution to their problems lay in the right to the ballot and, consequently, to expand the membership of the movement by appealing to them.

Bonnie J. Dow, "The *Revolution*, 1868–1870: Expanding the Woman Suffrage Agenda," in *A Voice of Their Own: The Woman Suffrage Press, 1840–1910*, ed. Martha M. Solomon, 1991.

included several prominent women, Stanton and Anthony were given relatively free rein in the NWSA's affairs. With *The Revolution* at their command, the two women seemed well equipped to plan special campaigns and to act quickly when the occasion demanded it.

Not everyone was pleased with the Stanton-Anthony leadership of the NWSA. William Lloyd Garrison, Wendell Phillips, Stephen and Abby Kelly Foster, and others believed that the two women had presumed too much in claiming to speak for all woman's movements and against the priority of Negro suffrage. The bitterness between the two factions was exacerbated by *The Revolution*'s ruthless criticism of those who disagreed with its policies:

> Their life boat is wrecked on the shoals; for they left the road-way of principle, shipped a cargo of expediency, and got their bottom barnacled with party fossils. Their estate is bankrupt; for they threw overboard their capital of conscience, consistency and courage.

The result of this rancor was the formation of a rival group, the American Woman Suffrage Association (AWSA). Formed by Lucy Stone and headquartered in Boston, the AWSA appealed to conservative suffragists. This group attracted a large membership despite the fact that it virtually was ignored by *The Revolution.*

Some suffragists remained loyal to Stanton, Anthony and *The Revolution.* Lydia Maria Child called herself an "unswerving friend." Paulina Wright Davis, editor of another suffrage newspaper, *Una*, gave the editors a generous sum of money. Phoebe and Alice Cary wrote for the paper and volunteered for office service. But Elizabeth Phelps was perhaps the greatest contributor. A rich and practical New York philanthropist, Phelps believed that there should be a rallying place in the city for women and their organizations. For this purpose, she bought a large elegant house and christened it the Woman's Bureau. Its rooms were rented solely to women's clubs and to enterprises conducted by women. *The Revolution* occupied the first

Lucy Stone

floor. When moving in, Anthony had warned Phelps that the newspaper's presence might adversely affect the popularity of the Woman's Bureau. She was right; the more conservative women and groups refused to use the house. And, after a year, Phelps abandoned the project, leaving *The Revolution* to find new quarters.

The end of the Woman's Bureau was not the end of *The Revolution*. It was alive and as spicy as ever. Concerned with everything that affected the nation's women, the newspaper covered female rights, financial matters, the political situation and the achievement of women in all phases of life.

A VARIETY OF INTERESTS

Of course, *The Revolution*'s primary interest was female enfranchisement. "Our pathway is straight to the ballot box, with no variableness nor shadow of turning," wrote Anthony. This pathway was strewn with constitutional road blocks. Thus, one of the major functions of *The Revolution* was to hammer away at the 14th and 15th amendments which gave the vote to the Negro but ignored women. The 15th amendment at best, said an editorial in *The Revolution*, was a trick of a "corrupt and unprincipled . . . school of politicians . . . to save themselves and their party. . . ."

Because this amendment was "invidious to their sex," *The Revolution*'s editors proposed a 16th amendment to the Constitution. This based the right of suffrage on citizenship which "all citizens of the United States, whether native or naturalized, shall enjoy . . . equally without any distinction or discrimination whatever founded on sex." In line with their 16th amendment, *The Revolution* promoted "educated suffrage." Since blacks in America were generally illiterate, educated suffrage favored voting women over voting Negroes. An editorial by Stanton explained:

> When I protest against . . . giving Jonathan, Patrick, and Sambo, and Hans, and Yang-Tang the power . . . to make the civil and moral codes for proud Saxon women, I am as sacredly defending human rights . . . as if I were straining every nerve to boost two million ignorant black men into legislators, judges and jurors.

The Revolution did more than complain about suffrage; it actively promoted the vote. The newspaper publicized suffrage meetings and lectures on woman's rights held throughout the country. It also reported the progress of the NWSA and solicited signatures for a woman suffrage petition to be sent to Congress. And it constantly refuted the religious, political, social and economic arguments against female enfranchisement. . . .

The vote was not only the woman's right for which *The Revolution* fought. There was little freedom for the female of 1868. Her property belonged to her father before she married, and her husband after. She had no legal control over her own children. And the large majority of schools and non-menial occupations were closed to her. "Bereft of their rights, education, and the wherewithall to be independent," said *The Revolution,* women were forced to prostitute themselves on the street and in marriage. The newspaper was against both forms of prostitution, especially the legal one. Stanton and Anthony were not opposed to marriage, but only to the institution as it then existed. Once wed, they claimed, a woman was essentially the property of her husband. She was treated like a brood sow, used by her spouse to "satiate his filthy lusts" and worked like a scullery maid. Only when women were the political equals of men, only when they had full control over their own persons could marriage be changed into an enriching, enobling, joyful experience.

Championing the right to women to any type of work or education, *The Revolution* trumpeted the accomplishments of females. The editors printed portraits of women clerks, jurors, physicians, postmasters, inventors and missionaries. Women of historical importance were also praised. No female deed seemed too small to merit the publication's attention. "Two women in Iowa," one story ran, "killed a wild deer with a fire shovel.". . .

TRAIN'S DEPARTURE

On the day of *The Revolution*'s debut, Train announced that he was going to England to promote business and engage European writers and subscribers for the newspaper. He did neither. Shortly after arriving in England, Train was arrested, ostensibly for not paying a $600 debt, but probably for his outspoken support of the Fenian movement. Train insisted that *The Revolution* had contributed to his downfall. British agents, reading the inflammatory name of the newspapers he carried, confiscated them as incriminating evidence.

Although incarcerated in Dublin for over a year, Train did not sever his connection with *The Revolution.* He kept up a lively correspondence, published in the newspaper and narrated his experiences in prison. But, when Train returned to the United States, this contribution ceased. In May 1869, *The Revolution* published a letter from Train stating he would no longer write for the publication and asking that his name not be mentioned in its pages. He noted that this move might bring the paper subscribers who had previously refused to support the publication because of his involvement. Despite this possibility, Stanton was sorry to see Train go. "He takes with him," she wrote, "the sincere thanks of those who know what he has done in the cause of women, and of those who appreciate what a power *The Revolution* has already been in raising the public thought to the importance of the speedy enfranchisement of women.". . .

A CHAMPION OF UNPOPULAR CAUSES

Economic and social issues always had concerned the editors of *The Revolution*. Their newspaper allowed them to champion causes which, although indisputedly connected with the crusade for woman's freedom, generally were ignored, even by other suffragists. One of these was the plight of the lower-class working woman. Thus, *The Revolution* called attention to women's substandard wages, demanded equal pay for equal work and an eight-hour day, supported unions and strikes, and called for an end to child labor. Only by the enactment of these reforms could women be freed from economic bondage and move toward equality with men.

The Revolution also supported the cause of other down-trodden individuals. Attempting to help the poor, the editors exposed the filthy conditions in the almshouses, jails and prisons. In its pages was the story of the wretched life in the tenement districts and a denunciation of slum landlords who thrived off poverty. The Indians' predicament was also publicized in *The Revolution,* which excoriated the "sane and sensible Christians" who either condoned or participated in the extermination of native Americans. And one poor immigrant girl, accused of killing her newborn child, actually was saved from the gallows by *The Revolution's* money and publicity.

Though all these positions were liberal for their time, *The Revolution's* concern with prostitution and abortion was considered radical. Abortion (delicately called "infanticide" by the editors) was, of course, deplored. But it was recognized as a product of bad conditions rather than of bad women. These conditions would be improved once the female had a more healthful life, an education and enfranchisement. The same cure was suggested for prostitution. But, until that evil could be eliminated, *The Revolution* said that prostitutes and their houses should be registered and regulated and that special hospitals be built to treat the diseases of the profession.

The Revolution was not all suffrage and suffering. It printed poems, book reviews and fictional stories. Publishing some of the finest American feminists and woman writers of the day—Anna Dickinson, Lucretia Mott, Matilda Joslyn Gage, Eleanor Kirk, Olive Logan and Lillie Devereaux Blake—the journal had a fine literary reputation. Well-known European women also contributed to the foreign correspondence section of every issue.

Out to save the world, *The Revolution* could not save itself. The publication was never financially solvent. There were few subscribers—about 3,000—because of the newspaper's reputation for radicalism and the fact that women had not been sufficiently aroused to support a publication of their own. There were not enough advertisers; the circulation was too small and composed of women who did not, as yet, make major purchasing decisions. Also, *The Revolution* reached few homes not already covered by the liberal New York *Tribune* or *Independent.* The subscription price of $2, and later $3, per year was not sufficient to support a weekly paper.

There was simply not enough money. *The Revolution,* printed on the best paper by high-salaried typesetters, was expensive to run, and Stanton and Anthony had neither the resources nor business acumen to run it. Train's promise of constant support was never kept. Contributions, although frequent and welcome, were not enough. But the spinster Anthony, whose child *The Revolution* had become, was determined to keep the newspaper alive. She "worked like a whole plantation of slaves," giving lectures, soliciting contributions, finding supporters and pouring every available cent into the publication. Anthony's family, who could ill afford it, even loaned her several thousand dollars.

A plan to save *The Revolution* was formulated in 1869. A stock company was to be established by several wealthy women, on a basis of $50,000, to relieve Anthony of all financial responsibility, making her simply the business manager. Isabella Beecher Hooker was anxious to keep the publication in print. She and her sister, Harriet Beecher Stowe, said they would give *The Revolution* their personal and financial support and the support of their large circle of friends. There was one condition attached: the editors must change the name of the paper to *"The True Republic,* or something equally satisfactory." Anthony did not want to comply, but she consulted with other newspaper editors and Stanton on the sagacity of the change. The newspapermen said that such a move was generally fatal to a publication. But, more importantly, Stanton considered it a great mistake. "A journal called *Rosebud,"* she said, "might answer for those who came with kid gloves and perfumes to lay immortal wreaths on the monuments others have built; but for us . . . there is no name like *REVOLUTION!"* Thus, the stock and the Beecher plans fell through and *The Revolution* received no contributions. It struggled into 1870 on its own.

The death blow to *The Revolution* was delivered by Stanton's and Anthony's old Boston rivals. Led by Lucy Stone and her husband Henry Blackwell, the group founded its own newspaper in 1870. Their *Woman's Journal* was placed on a sound financial basis from the very beginning. Not dependent on a temperamental "angel," it was a real business conducted in the best Boston tradition of trusteeships, annuity systems, family trusts and sound funding. Mary A. Livermore, publisher of the *Agitator,* another suffrage newspaper, was persuaded by Stone to merge her work with the *Woman's Journal* and come to Boston to serve as its editor. This new publication had not only Boston money and Livermore experience, but also a greater audience. Being more conservative than its New York sister, the *Woman's Journal* attracted those who were in favor of woman's rights but could not accept the wide ranging radical reforms proposed by *The Revolution.*

THE END NEARS

Faced with financial difficulties and the stronger *Journal, The Revolution* could not survive long. Theodore Tilton, a stalwart friend of the newspaper and a liberal journalist himself, encouraged Laura Curtis Bullard to take *The Revolution* off the editors' tired hands. A wealthy suffragist possessed of some literary ability, Bullard bought the publication in June, 1870 for the nominal sum of one dollar. Anthony assumed sole responsibility for the paper's debt of

$10,000. Stanton had seven children to care for; Anthony had only *The Revolution*. Thus, the spinster was crushed by the loss of the publication. Signing the transfer, she said in her diary, was "like signing my own death warrant." And, to a friend she wrote, "I feel a great calm sadness like that of a mother binding out a dear child she could not support."

Bullard's journal, which she published for 18 months, was *The Revolution* in name only. Hers was an inoffensive literary and social journal, adding such new features as the "Children's Corner," "Houshold" (sic), recipes and fashions. Political material was still published, but it was nearly lost amidst "kitchen and parlor" news.

Sold to the New York *Christian Enquirer* in 1872, *The Revolution* disappeared even in name. It was such a short life for such a lively publication. But it was not a life without meaning. The newspaper made a considerable contribution to the nation's women and to the suffrage movement and its press. *The Revolution* championed many unpopular causes in the area of woman's and human rights. It brought attention to the plight of the immigrant, the poor and the lower-class working woman. It promoted the professional, political, cultural, financial and educational advancement of the female and discussed prostitution, abortion and illegitimacy with a sympathy few other publications evidenced. The paper also served the movement by its stalwart insistence on woman suffrage in the "Negro's hour." *The Revolution* publicized and propagandized enfranchisement and kept it in the forefront of public attention. At a time when the country was in turmoil, the movement divided, and the cause confused, *The Revolution* carried on the idea of woman's full and equal participation in all phases of American life.

But, perhaps the greatest contribution of *The Revolution* was not to its present, but to its future. The newspaper set down for the first time in a major national forum arguments for women's equality that are still being used. And it began a century-long tradition of women's political journalism. *The Revolution* inspired the establishment of several contemporaneous suffrage publications, including the *Woman's Tribune* and the *Agitator*. Mary Livermore, editor of the latter, said she intended her paper to be "nothing more or less than the twin sister of *The Revolution*, whose mission is to turn everything inside out." The Stanton-Anthony paper also prompted the creation of the *Woman's Journal*, the most important suffrage publication, that was to run until 1932. Today we find a child, a great-granddaughter, of *The Revolution* in *Ms.*

Even in her own time, Susan B. Anthony realized the importance of the contribution she, Elizabeth Cady Stanton, and *The Revolution* had made to suffrage journalism. In a letter to a friend, she said,

> None but the good Father can ever begin to know the terrible struggle of those years. I am not complaining, for mine is but the fate of almost every originator or pioneer who has ever opened up a way. I have the joy of knowing that I showed it to be possible to publish an out-and-out woman's paper, and taught other women to enter in to reap where I have sown.

The Trade Union Career of Susan B. Anthony

Israel Kugler

The following essay by Israel Kugler traces Susan B. Anthony's brief involvement with the labor movement that arose after the Civil War. Disillusioned by the Republicans' betrayal of women's suffrage and finding little support among the Democrats, Anthony turned to the National Labor Union, which was quickly becoming a powerful political force. Kugler writes that Anthony helped to organize trade unions for working women, especially among the female typesetters who were employed by the *Revolution*, her suffragist newspaper.

However, he states, Anthony's commitment to the principles of the labor movement and to improving the conditions faced by working women was not as strong as her desire to win new converts to women's suffrage among the working class. Kugler describes how she ran afoul of the labor movement during a strike of male printers, when she urged women to fill the strikers' places in order to learn the trade. Anthony believed she was offering the women a chance to improve their skills, the author explains, but the union leaders understandably condemned her actions as strikebreaking. In Kugler's opinion, Anthony primarily saw the labor movement as an expedient tool to further her ultimate goal of obtaining suffrage for women.

Kugler is a professor emeritus in social science at the City University of New York and the author of *From Ladies to Women: The Organized Struggle for Woman's Rights in the Reconstruction Era.*

The 19th Amendment has rightfully been called the Susan B. Anthony section of the Constitution. No other person had la-

From "The Trade Union Career of Susan B. Anthony," by Israel Kugler, *Labor History*, Winter 1961, www.tandf.co.uk/journals. Reprinted with permission.

bored so hard on behalf of woman's suffrage. The little known phase of Miss Anthony's life as a participant in the trade union movement gives us a sharper insight into her basic outlook.

THE BACKGROUND

Prior to the Civil War, middle class, educated women participated in the reform currents, from abolition to temperance, that rippled across the country. These women deeply resented the secondary roles assigned them by men, and they formed associations dedicated to woman's rights. The Civil War swallowed up all these reform organizations in the great national effort to defeat the Confederacy.

After the war was over, the concept of Reconstruction meant to the reformers the dawn of a new day when all their ideals would become realities. The woman's righters sought to make common cause with the abolitionists in the hope that the amendments granting citizenship and suffrage would apply to all women as well as to all men. The Radical Republicans, however, wanted to restrict these amendments to males. They felt that the controversial question of woman suffrage would complicate matters. Besides, male suffrage for Negroes was enough to guarantee the Republicans political control of the Congress.

This situation created a deep cleavage within the woman's rights movement. The abolitionist-oriented moderates led by Lucy Stone agreed that this was "the Negro's hour" and somewhat regretfully supported the 14th and 15th Amendments. Miss Anthony and her colleague, Elizabeth Cady Stanton, claimed priority for woman suffrage and were ready to make common cause with members of any group, even those that were opposed to Negro suffrage.

This outlook led Susan B. Anthony to join forces with a wealthy reformer—eccentric George Francis Train. He offered to finance for Miss Anthony a newspaper called *The Revolution.* Soon after its initial publication, Train was off on an Irish independence junket in Britain, where he was jailed, and the paper became entirely dependent on Miss Anthony's resources. Because of her connection with Train, who opposed Negro suffrage, Miss Anthony was eliminated from the leadership of the American Equal Rights Association. She organized another suffrage organization, dedicated to granting suffrage to "educated" citizens, and continued to publish *The Revolution.*

This newspaper, advocating as it did the eight-hour day, equal pay for equal work, more organized labor, met with support from the labor reform papers, especially the Chicago *Workingman's Advocate,* the official organ of the National Labor Union. The daily press and the abolitionist wing of the woman's rights movement ridiculed *The Revolution* unmercifully.

SEARCHING FOR NEW ALLIES

By 1868, Susan B. Anthony was thoroughly out of sympathy with a policy of blind subservience to the Republican party. She was determined to explore the possibilities of getting woman suffrage into the platforms of both major parties. Failing that, she was ready to consider merging with other reform elements to put forth a new party.

The young labor movement grew in strength parallel to the rapid strides of Northern industry during the Civil War. At the end of the war, the addition of the returning soldiers to the labor market helped create a desire for national reform and the merging of the separate national trade unions. This was the basis for the formation of the National Labor Union (NLU) in 1866.

The NLU soon claimed to have over 600,000 adherents. It had obtained an audience with President Andrew Johnson and secured the passage of a law establishing the eight-hour day in government navy yards and arsenals. The leadership of the NLU, particularly William Sylvis and Richard Trevellick, was most sympathetic to woman suffrage, equal pay for equal work, and the organization of women into trade unions.

Miss Anthony's preparations for the 1868 Democratic party convention in Tammany Hall included a conference with David Meliss, the financial editor of the *New York World,* and J. C. Whaley, the President of the National Labor Union. Her proposals, agreed to by the NLU, were read to the Democratic convention. They were greeted by jeers and laughter. The Republican convention that same year refused to grant her proposals a hearing.

Having been rejected by the abolitionist-moderates in the woman's rights movement, and ignored and ridiculed by the two major parties, there seemed to be only one course open: to join with the National Labor Union; to push it in the direction of independent political action; to organize women into unions. This new and powerful force could be oriented toward woman's rights.

When the 1868 call to the National Labor Convention went out, inviting unions and all organizations which worked for the "amelioration of the condition of those who labor for a living," Susan B. Anthony seized the opportunity to get representation at the convention for the militant woman's righters. Mrs. Mary MacDonald, who owned some property in Mount Vernon, New York, called a meeting of other women property owners who wanted to vote on tax and school matters. They organized themselves into the "Woman's Suffrage and Protective Labor Association of Mount Vernon" and voted to join the National Labor Union.

Two days later on September 17, 1868, Miss Anthony called a meeting in the offices of *The Revolution* to form a workingwomen's association "for the purpose of doing everything possible to elevate women and raise the value of their labor." The women typesetters and clerks employed by *The Revolution,* together with Mrs. Stanton, Mrs. MacDonald and Miss Anthony, formed the membership of this association. They rejected woman suffrage as part of their program. Miss Anthony and Mrs. Stanton were indulgent and went along with this slap at their favorite social panacea. Miss Anthony was elected a delegate to the NLU convention.

At the Workingwomen's Home, a boarding house located at 45 Elizabeth Street in New York City, another meeting was held and Mary Kellogg Putnam, the daughter of Edward Kellogg, the monetary reformer, was elected as the third delegate. Mrs. Stanton presented her credentials from the Woman's Suffrage Association of America as the fourth delegate in the woman's entourage to the National Labor Union convention.

The convention itself, which was held on September 21, 1868, was extremely cordial to the women delegates. By and large the convention delegates were willing to stretch a point and seat them as accredited participants. It must be remembered that the "organizations" they purported to represent were developed overnight. The woman's righters could scarcely be considered as workingwomen. . . .

The woman delegates participated actively. They were on key committees and caucused in attempts to get women elected to NLU office. They succeeded in getting Kate Mullaney of the Troy Collar Workers Union elected as Second Vice-President. This had to be annulled because the First Vice-President came from the same state. She was given the high post of Assistant Secretary of the National Labor Union. . . .

There was abundant evidence of virtually point-by-point agreement between the woman's righters and the program of the National Labor Union. Equal pay for equal work and organization of women were heartily endorsed. . . . The one exception was woman suffrage. Susan Anthony and her colleagues were so pleased to be integrated into a viable organization representing 600,000 workers that they were willing to overlook the lack of support for woman's votes. . . .

The convention passed a resolution that recognized Miss Anthony's paper *The Revolution* as "an able and well-conducted advocate of our principle. . . ." It called "upon men and women of all occupations to render it full and impartial support."

ORGANIZING WOMEN WORKERS

Miss Anthony invited the delegates to attend meetings of the newly formed Workingwomen's Associations that were to be held in the evening following the close of the convention sessions.

One of the Association meetings had as its aim the organization of a Woman's Typographical Union.

> Mr. Alexander Troup, a delegate to the National Labor Congress from Typographical Union No. 6 denied that the association of which he was a member was in hostility to the female compositors. If the female compositors will work together with the members of the Union, they will get equal remuneration for their labor.

> Miss Peers—Will the union allow ladies to join their ranks as members?

> Mr. Troup—I never knew of any woman applying for admission. I can speak for Mr. McKechnie, the present foreman of the *World* and President of the National Typographical Union as being in favor of women working at case with equal rights and privileges as the men. But he is not in favor, nor am I of women coming in to undermine the prices paid to men.

> Miss Anthony—How much is the initiation in this union of yours?

> Mr. Troup—One Dollar.

> Miss Anthony—Oh, that is not much; I guess our girls can

stand that. (Laughter)

Miss Peers to Mr. Troup—Will you take my initiation fee now, if you please?

Mr. Troup—Yes of course I shall; and will propose you as a member.

This report of the organizing of the Woman's Typographical Union was but the first of several successful attempts to draw women into unions. Miss Anthony addressed its first formal meeting with these words:

> Girls, you must take this matter to heart seriously now, for you have established a union, and for the first time in woman's history in the United States you are placed, and by your own efforts, on a level with men, as far as possible, to obtain wages for your labor. I need not say that you have taken a great momentous step forward in the path to success. Keep at it now girls, and you will achieve full and plenteous success. (Applause)

A report was read that the proprietors of *Flake's Bulletin* of Galveston, Texas wished to have the Woman's Typographical Union send a woman compositor but at a rate of pay below that paid to men. Miss Anthony vigorously supported Gussie Lewis, the union president, in rejecting this offer. . . .

Susan B. Anthony continued to organize workers into unions in the immediate period following the convention. First came the garment workers and then the sewing machine operators. All organizing meetings included the plea for woman suffrage and for the founding of cooperative workshops.

The Workingwomen's Associations merged and met in the offices of *The Revolution.* The meetings toward the end of the year began to veer away from the staggering task of organizing women workers. Instead, the emphasis was placed on fact-finding investigations into the conditions in various industries employing women. Lectures were devoted to temperance, fashion, marriage and divorce. The actual women who worked for a living began to drift from the Association. It became an uplift organization with a sympathetic labor orientation. The women who came were middle-class intellectuals.

The Revolution had long exhausted the funds that Train had initially advanced. A deficit was mounting. Miss Anthony had to go on frequent lecture tours to get the funds that would keep the paper from collapsing. The fact that the independent labor reform political organization did not materialize for the presidential elections of 1868 was most disappointing to Miss Anthony. She returned more and more to the idea of concentrating efforts calculated to bring public attention to all phases of the social status of women.

The National Labor Union convention held in August, 1869 was the scene of a protracted struggle against accepting the credentials of Susan B. Anthony as a delegate. The background for this scene was a series of events that began in the spring of that year and which symbolized the basic divergence in outlook between Miss Anthony and the organized labor movement.

The NLU had grown larger and more powerful under the expert leadership of William Sylvis. Prior to the 1869 convention, Sylvis died and his place was taken by Richard Trevellick. Both Trevellick and Sylvis were friendly to Miss Anthony, but Sylvis had immense support among the trade union leaders and Trevellick could not match his qualities of leadership.

A PROTEST AGAINST ANTHONY

When Susan Anthony appeared at the convention, her credentials were challenged by delegate Walsh of the Typographical Union No. 6 of New York:

> I am directed by Typographical Union No. 6 comprising 2000 members to protest in their names the admission of Miss Susan B. Anthony. We claim that she is not a friend of labor. I understand that the lady is here to represent a Workingwomen's Association of New York, composed of male and female agitators in a movement for female suffrage. I oppose her admission on the ground that she is a determined enemy of labor. . . . In the first place, the lady is proprietor of a paper published in New York, called *The Revolution,* and while the columns of that paper proclaim the principle of equal wages for men and women, its forms are gotten out by as notorious 'rats' as we have in our trade, and who are opposed to our organization at every point. The ladies working on that paper do not receive the same wages men receive, and this, too notwithstanding the officers of our Union under the direction of that body called upon the proprietor of that paper and requested her to observe the same scale of prices which was observed in a union office. In the second place, during the struggle with their employers in which Typographical Union No. 6 was engaged last spring—a struggle which cost us $24,000—a meeting of our employers was held at Astor House and the lady . . . waited on those employers and solicited aid to furnish a room wherein females could learn to set type, thereby enabling our employers to defeat our just demands by throwing upon the market unskilled labor. . . . This

is not a place for any but those who work and who know our wants and the disadvantages under which we labor.

We, therefore protest against the admission of the lady, and trust that every man here who knows what strikes are and who is a member of a trade union will stand by us on this question. If they do not I can see no good in this organization. If enemies and friends alike are to be admitted we do not want to be here. We represent a large membership, pay a large tax, struggle hard for our principles, and I trust that no one who is not a genuine friend of labor will be admitted here.

Miss Anthony defended herself against these charges insisting:

1. That she didn't know that Johnston, her printer, was anti-union.

2. That the girls employed were paid more than in any other printshop in the city.

3. That it is true that during the printers' strike she asked the employers to help her set up a type-setting school to train replacements.

Miss Anthony freely stated:

. . . they (the employers) concluded to open schools themselves and promised to take girls to learn the trade, and I said to the girls who applied to me by fifties, go in and learn your trade. I knew full well that when Union No. 6 came in line with the employers, or the employers with them, the girls would be turned adrift; but I said to myself, they will have acquired a little education, a little help, and I will have helped them this much. The result was that some forty or fifty girls served with Gray and Green and others, during a few months while the strike was in progress. . . .

The printers further charged that Miss Anthony knew Augusta Lewis, the President of Woman Typographical Union No. 1, had been fired from *The Revolution* staff for union activity. This charge was denied by Miss Anthony.

The first vote on her being seated was very close: 55 to 52 in her favor. Miss Anthony was ably championed by labor reform delegates and the shoemakers' union, the Knights of St. Crispin.

At this point a resolution of Typographical Union No. 6 was read to the convention substantiating the charge that Susan B. Anthony did indeed participate in the firing of Miss Lewis and that in fact *The Revolution* was paying less than union scale wages. The delegate from the union threatened to withdraw from the convention if she were seated.

In her final defense before the convention, Miss Anthony

claimed that the real reason why the delegates opposed seating her was that women did not have the right to vote. If women had the franchise, they would be respected, admitted to the trade and treated with equality.

It remained for Miss Anthony's colleague, Elizabeth Cady Stanton to point up the divergence between the trades-union movement and the woman's righters:

> Miss Anthony, hanging by the eyelids four days in a Workingman's Convention, has given the press a grand opportunity to manifest the manly elements of justice and chivalry. ... The result has proved what *The Revolution* has said again and again, that the worst enemies of Woman's Suffrage will ever be the laboring classes of men. ... Their late action towards Miss Anthony is but the expression of the hostility they feel to the idea she represents.

The final vote of 63 to 28 against seating Miss Anthony marked the end of collaboration between the middle class woman's rights reformers and the organized labor movement in the Reconstruction period.

ANTHONY'S SINGLE-MINDED PURPOSE

As the ardent champion of woman's rights, Miss Anthony was ready to unite with any group that could further her purpose. She was equally ready to part with that group if her monomanic cause could be served by betraying the very principles on which an erstwhile ally stood. Susan B. Anthony's trade union career was a short-lived, opportunist adventure, an interesting episode in her tireless campaign for woman's rights.

Susan B. Anthony Cast Her Ballot for Ulysses S. Grant

Godfrey D. Lehman

After the passage of the Fourteenth and Fifteenth Amendments, several feminists noticed that the wording of the amendments could be interpreted as guaranteeing women's right to vote. Susan B. Anthony decided to test this interpretation by going to the polls during the presidential election of November 1872. As Godfrey D. Lehman relates in the following article, the election officials allowed Anthony to cast her ballot, but she was subsequently arrested and charged with voting illegally. Lehman provides a vivid account of the court case, especially concerning the judicial irregularities that led many observers to believe Anthony did not receive a fair trial. A specialist on juries, Lehman has published numerous articles on jurors' rights and the book *We the Jury . . . The Impact of Jurors on Our Basic Freedoms.*

Shortly before the Republicans convened in Philadelphia in 1872 to renominate Ulysses S. Grant for President, Susan Brownell Anthony visited him at the White House. She told the President that her National Woman Suffrage Association (NWSA) wanted him to make votes for women a plank in his platform. Grant replied that he had "already done more for women than any other president." He recognized the "right of women to be postmasters," he said, and had named five thousand to the post, but he would make no promises about the party platform.

PARTY POLITICS

Anthony had never been comfortable playing the role of supplicant. The NWSA's mottoes avoided any pleading tone:

Excerpted from "Susan B. Anthony Cast Her Ballot for Ulysses S. Grant," by Godfrey D. Lehman, *American Heritage,* December 1985. Reprinted with permission from *American Heritage.*

"Men—their rights and nothing more. Women—their rights and nothing less"; "Principle, not Policy. Justice, not Favors." But the suffragists believed that Republicans were their best bet in the upcoming election; Henry Wilson, who was to be Grant's vice-presidential running mate, was less equivocal about women's suffrage than Grant, while Horace Greeley, the probable Democratic candidate, was outspokenly against it.

Anthony had asked for Greeley's support five years earlier. "The bullet and the ballot go together, madam," he had replied. "If you vote, are you prepared to fight?" "Yes, Mr. Greeley. Just as you fought in the late war—at the point of a goose quill." The answer hardly endeared her cause to him, and Greeley had not changed his position in the intervening years; he had stated publicly that "the best women I know do not want to vote."

She knew better than to expect much progress, however, when she arrived in Philadelphia for the Republican convention on Friday, June 7. The NWSA delegation was met, as often before, with gallant words and the excuse of "party expediency." Anthony was told that the chief objective of the convention was to ensure full citizenship and voting rights for the "colored male citizen." Distractions would have to be postponed. Anthony had fought against slavery for years, but she rejected an application of the Thirteenth Amendment that left black and white women alike enslaved to male relatives.

In the end, Anthony's delegation had to accept a campaign plank that soothingly cited Republican "obligations to the loyal women of America for their noble devotion to the cause of freedom" and the hope for "their admission to wider fields of usefulness." Nevertheless, the plank ended with the statement, "The honest demands of any class of citizens for equal rights should be treated with respectful consideration." No national party had said even that much before.

Having decided to throw her organization's support to the Republicans, Anthony started a speaking tour on September 20. She was convinced "without a particle of doubt" that, in fact, the Constitution already guaranteed women's right to vote. The new Fourteenth and Fifteenth Amendments assured it. The Fourteenth, just four years old, decreed that "all persons born or naturalized in the United States . . . are citizens" and "no State shall make or enforce any law which shall abridge the privileges or immunities of citizens." The

Fifteenth, added in 1870, prohibited any state from withholding the right to vote from any citizen "on account of race, color, or previous condition of servitude." The suffragists had lobbied to include the word *sex*, but again, the excuse of "party expediency" had prevailed. Nonetheless there could be no justifiable doubt because the Fourteenth also included the caveat that no state could deny "to any person . . . the equal protection of the laws." Totally convinced of women's constitutional right to vote, Anthony decided to present herself to the board of registry on the designated date; on Election Day, she would cast her ballot.

Two territories had already recognized women's voting rights: Wyoming in 1869 and Utah in 1870. Nor would Anthony be the first woman to attempt to vote in one of the states. Marilla M. Ricker of Dover, New Hampshire, had been rebuffed in 1870, but in April of 1871 Nanette B. Gardner voted in Detroit and got away with it. That same month seventy-two women had tried to register in the District of Columbia but had been denied. When they had appealed to the supreme court of the district, the judges proclaimed that the granting of citizenship did not necessarily confer the right to vote, thereby ignoring several law dictionaries that defined citizenship as including the "right to vote . . . for public officers." The United States Supreme Court saw no reason to overturn the lower court's decision.

Several other voting attempts had been frustrated at one level or another, but Mrs. L.D. Mansfield and "three other ladies" had registered and succeeded in voting in Nyack, New York, in 1871. "No evil results followed," *The New York Times* concluded in an editorial.

REGISTERING TO VOTE

Anthony sought substantiation for her decision to vote from lawyers in her hometown of Rochester, New York, but none was interested until she called upon Henry R. Selden, a former judge of the New York Court of Appeals and of the state supreme court. Like the others, Selden had never considered the issue, but he agreed to review it. After doing so, he told Anthony the amendments did guarantee voting rights to women. He promised to support her claim.

Anthony was pleased, but she had already decided to proceed whatever his opinion. On Friday, November 1, when the Rochester *Democrat and Chronicle* urged all citizens to

"Register NOW," Anthony gathered fifteen other women, including her three sisters, and appeared that very day before a startled board of registry in a barbershop in Rochester's Eighth Ward.

Two members of the three-man board, Beverly Jones and Edwin F. Marsh, were Republicans; the third was a Democrat named William B. Hall. Anthony offered her credentials, and Jones, chief of the board, sought the advice of his superiors. Two U.S. supervisors of elections had been appointed to oversee things in the Eighth Ward, but one left the barbershop as soon as the women entered. The other could see no way to get around placing the names in the register; he asked if Jones knew the penalty for refusing to register an eligible voter.

This convinced Jones and Marsh, but Hall resisted. The 2 to 1 majority prevailed, however, and all the women were registered. When the Rochester newspapers published the story the next day, some thirty-five other women came to register in other wards. Their action was denounced by the Rochester *Union and Advertiser*, which demanded the prosecution of any election official who accepted their ballots. The paper published the essential features of an enforcement act of the Fourteenth Amendment: "Any person . . . who shall vote without having a legal right to vote; or do any unlawful act to secure . . . an opportunity to vote for himself or any other person . . . shall be deemed guilty of a crime," punishable by a fine of five hundred dollars and/or imprisonment up to three years. This warning was so intimidating that on Election Day, November 5, no official in any ward except the Eighth permitted women to vote.

The sixteen registered women of the Eighth Ward arrived as the polls opened at seven o'clock: they found the same three men there, now serving as inspectors of election. The women asked for ballots, they received them, and they all voted. Most of the ballots were returned to Jones or Marsh, but even Hall accepted some. The women went home, the ballots were counted, and the story was telegraphed across the nation.

On Thanksgiving Day, Thursday, November 28, an imposingly tall, impeccably attired, and very fidgety gentleman presented himself at the Anthony family's front door. After a few nervous comments about the weather he began hesitantly, "Miss Anthony," but could not continue.

"Won't you sit down?" she said pleasantly.

"No thank you. You see, Miss Anthony . . ," he stammered. "I am here on a most uncomfortable errand." He hesitated again. "The fact is, Miss Anthony . . . I have come to arrest you." The unhappy deputy marshal, E.J. Keeney, seemed about to collapse, but he pressed on. "If you will oblige me by coming as soon as possible to the District Attorney's office, no escort will be necessary."

"Is this the usual manner of serving a warrant?"

Keeney blushed and drew the warrant from his pocket. It said she had violated an act of Congress.

The possibility of arrest had never occurred to Anthony, but she kept her composure. "I prefer to be arrested like anybody else. You may handcuff me as soon as I get my coat and hat." Keeney refused.

The marshal then served warrants on her three sisters; in other parts of the city, deputies were calling on the twelve other women. The sixteen were brought into a bleak, dirty courtroom where only a few years before runaway slaves had been held awaiting trial. No one acknowledged their presence until early evening, when the commissioner of elections arrived to inform them that the district attorney had failed to appear; they could go home and return the following morning.

On Friday Anthony was subjected to an inquisition:

"Would you have made the same efforts to vote that you did, if you had not consulted with Judge Selden?"

"Yes, sir," she replied.

"Were you influenced in the matter by his advice at all?"

"No, sir."

"You went into this matter for the purpose of testing the question?"

"Yes, sir; I had been resolved for three years to vote at the first election when I had been at home for thirty days before."

The hearing had aroused so much interest that crowds of women came to witness it, and the proceedings were moved to a larger, cleaner room. One local newspaper described "these lawbreakers" as "elderly, matronly-looking women, with thoughtful faces, just the sort one would like to see in charge of one's sick room, considerate, patient, kindly." Actually Anthony was fifty-two, and many of the others were younger; all but three were married. They pleaded not guilty and, placed under bail of five hundred dollars each, were ordered to appear before a grand jury in Albany on January 22, 1873. On that date the twenty grand jurors swore that "the said Susan B. Anthony, being then and there a person of the female sex [which] she well knew . . . on the 5th day of November, 1872 . . . did knowingly and unlawfully vote," which she "well knew" was unlawful. The indictment was signed by Richard Crowley, United States attorney.

The three inspectors were indicted for registering and later accepting the ballots, although William B. Hall, a Democrat, protested vainly he had been against it and should be excluded. Anthony asked Judge Selden to represent her, and he did without fee; he was joined by the attorney John

Van Voorhis. A vindictive district judge, Nathan Hall, set Anthony's bail at an abnormally high one thousand dollars. (At that time a family could live a whole year on a thousand dollars.) She refused to pay, electing jail, but Selden, unwilling to see his client go to prison, put up the money.

After she left the courtroom, Van Voorhis informed her that because she did not go to jail she had just lost the right to appeal to the U.S. Supreme Court.

Ulysses S. Grant

Anthony rushed back into the courtroom and asked Selden to withdraw the bail, but it was too late. The bail had been recorded. A jury trial was set for June 17, 1873, in Rochester. The government decided to prosecute her alone as representative of the sixteen. And all three inspectors were ordered to trial on June 18, over William B. Hall's protests.

MAKING HER CASE

Anthony now took her case directly to the people of Rochester's Monroe County—her prospective jurors. In those pretelephone days the district post offices were important gathering places where newspapers from other cities arrived first, where people came to gossip and exchange news, and where speakers could almost always find a crowd eager to hear their messages. Between her indictment and late May, Anthony appeared at all twenty-nine post offices in the county, sending posters on ahead to advertise each lecture. She told her audiences that "I not only committed no crime, but instead simply exercised my citizen's right, guaranteed to me and all United States citizens by the National Constitution, beyond the power of any state to deny." Those "grand documents"—the Declaration of Independence and the United States Constitution—do not delegate to government the "power to create or confer rights" but "propose to protect the people in the exercise of their God-given rights." The constitutions of every one of the then existing thirty-six states are "all alike" in that "not one of them pretends to bestow rights." There is "no shadow of governmental authority over rights, nor exclusion of any class from their full and equal enjoyment." She drew from the Declaration the phrase that rights are "unalienable" and that governments were formed only "to secure these rights," not to grant what was inherent.

It was contrary to true constitutionalism, she asserted, that one-half of the people should be subjugated to the other half through a "hateful oligarchy of sex." Women were compelled to pay taxes without representation; were brought to trial "without a jury of their peers," imprisoned, and even hanged; were robbed in marriage of the custody of their own wages, their own children, their own persons. "We, the people" did not mean "We, the white male citizens" or even "We, the male citizens" but "We, the whole people," and it "is a downright mockery to talk to women of their enjoyment of the blessings of liberty" while they are denied the ballot.

Anthony covered the county so well that, by May, Prosecutor Crowley was worried that no Monroe County jury would convict her. He carried this complaint to Judge Nathan Hall in Albany and requested moving the trial to the more remote town of Canandaigua. Hall readily complied, and only twenty-two days before the trial date he imposed additional costs and burdens on the defendants by requiring the twenty-eight-mile journey from Rochester.

Nothing seems to have been recorded about whether Anthony or the inspectors remained in Canandaigua throughout the period or commuted. In any case, Anthony made twenty-one appearances before the trial speaking on the subject "Is It a Crime for a United States Citizen to Vote?" Her friend Matilda Joslyn Gage traveled with her and gave her speech, "The United States on Trial, Not Susan B. Anthony," sixteen times. The two women appeared together on the evening of June 16. The next day, Susan B. Anthony went on trial.

THE PROCEEDINGS OF THE TRIAL

At 2:30 P.M. a jury was impaneled "without difficulty," *The New York Times* reported. The government used one peremptory challenge, and the defense three. Nothing else is recorded about this jury, although an enormous issue was to rest with them. Although every other participant in the trial is identified, no record survives of how the basic venire was chosen. But since New York jurors had to be "male inhabitants" between twenty-one and sixty who owned personal property assessed at $250 or greater or a "freehold estate" belonging to them or their wives valued at $150, it is safe to assume that Anthony's jury was composed of fairly wealthy, well-established men.

The courtroom in Canandaigua was crowded, with former President Millard Fillmore among the spectators. Selden asked Judge Nathan Hall to sit together with the presiding judge, despite his prejudice, because he believed it would be impossible to make an appeal on reversible error to a higher court with only a single judge. Hall refused.

It was evident almost from the first "Hear ye, hear ye" of the bailiff that Judge Ward Hunt, a Supreme Court justice and former mayor of Utica, New York, had allied himself with Crowley. Early in the trial Hunt refused to permit Anthony to be a witness in her own behalf, ruling she was "incompetent." But he did allow Assistant U.S. District Attorney John E. Pound to offer hearsay evidence concerning testimony she had given at pretrial hearings. Judge Selden protested: this would be "the version which the United States office took of her evidence," and if Anthony was given no chance to reply, it should be excluded. At this objection Hunt delivered a two-word directive to Pound: "Go on."

But Hunt did permit Selden to offer himself as a witness. Selden told the jury of his background of some dozen years as a judge, and how, after scholarly research, he had informed Anthony that she had a constitutionally guaranteed right to vote. He still believed it beyond any doubt, he said, and Anthony's acting on it indicated she was only following in good faith a constitutional mandate; therefore, she could not possibly have "knowingly" voted "unlawfully."

Crowley, for the prosecution, addressed the jury at some

length. There was no law permitting women to vote, Crowley said, and not knowing this was no excuse. A "good faith" defense was "abhorrent," even though Crowley himself had written the word *knowingly* into the indictment.

A CRUCIAL TURNING POINT

Nancy A. Hewitt is a professor of history at Rutgers University in New Brunswick, New Jersey. In the following piece, Hewitt maintains that Anthony's trial marked a decisive turn in the direction of the women's rights movement. From this point on, she writes, the movement began to focus more narrowly on obtaining women's suffrage at the expense of the more radical goals of the early feminists.

Anthony's trial was a turning point in the woman's rights movement, the starting point of its transition into the woman's suffrage movement. The new cause was radical in its attack on the most well-protected bastion of male privilege—political office—yet conservative in its acceptance of the existing power structure so long as women were allowed equal access to its benefits. Anthony's stirring rhetoric of Revolutionary [War] antecedents and Godly admonitions appealed more strongly to other female activists, particularly as her goal was the specific one of suffrage, than had ultraists' earlier appeals for a revolution in social, sexual, and familial relations.

Nancy A. Hewitt, *Women's Activism and Social Change: Rochester, New York, 1822–1872,* 1984.

Selden knew he faced heavy odds. His closing argument consumed nearly three hours. He put three propositions to the jury:

1. Was the defendant legally entitled to vote at the election in question?
2. If she were not entitled to vote, but believed that she was, and voted in good faith in that belief, did such voting constitute a crime under the statute before referred to?
3. Did the defendant vote in good faith and belief?

Selden argued that all just government rests upon the principles that "every citizen has a right to take part upon equal terms with every other citizen" and that inherent in citizenship is the right to vote. He quoted from the dictionaries that the court of the District of Columbia had shunned the previous year.

Since women were citizens, having been born or naturalized within the meaning of the Fourteenth Amendment, it followed they had the right to vote. Otherwise, they would be held
in "absolute political bondage"—in short, "slavery." One of the
chief arguments in the senatorial debates on the Fourteenth
Amendment four years earlier, was that the amendment
would "protect every citizen, black or white, male or female."

At the very worst, Selden continued, if he had been mis-
taken and there were no right, Anthony had acted in good
faith, and so the charge that she "knowingly" violated the
Constitution must be void. "It is incumbent on the prosecution to show affirmatively that she voted knowing she had
no right to vote. The essence of the offense is that it is done
with a knowledge that it is without right.

"Knowingly was inserted," Judge Selden went on, "to furnish security against the inability of stupid or prejudiced
judges or jurors to distinguish between wilful wrong and innocent mistake. An innocent mistake is not a crime. An innocent mistake, whether of law or fact, can never constitute
a crime." Judge Hunt tolerated all this because he had the
last say. He read a "brief statement" he had written *before* the
trial had started—before any evidence, before Selden had
presented any defense, any arguments, or points of law:
"The question before the jury is wholly a question or questions of law [and] under the 14th Amendment . . . Miss Anthony was not protected in a right to vote. And I have decided
also that her belief and the advice which she took does not
protect her in the act she committed. If I am right in this, the
result must be a verdict on your part of 'guilty,' and therefore
I direct that you find a verdict of 'guilty.'"

The people in the courtroom gasped. Selden jumped to
his feet. "That is a direction no court has the power to make
in a criminal case," he said incredulously.

Ignoring him, Hunt turned to the clerk. "Take the verdict,
Mr. Clerk."

The clerk addressed the jury: "Hearken to your verdict as
the court has recorded it. You say you find the defendant guilty
of the offense whereof she stands indicted, and so say you all?"

Not a juror responded.

Selden demanded the jury be polled, but Hunt shut him
off, saying, "No, gentlemen of the jury, you are discharged,"
and he adjourned the court. The finale was acted out so
quickly that it seemed rehearsed.

The twelve jurors sat stunned and confused in the box. During the entire proceedings they had uttered not a word, but now, quizzed by the defense and the press, they voiced frustration and outrage. Many complained this was not their verdict at all; they had not responded to the clerk simply because they didn't know they could. It was clear that the sentiment of the panel was to acquit.

THE RIGHT TO A TRIAL BY JURY

Hunt's arbitrary action altered the entire character of the trial. No longer was the issue women suffrage alone; it was now the question of the fundamental right to trial by an impartial jury. Many newspapers across the country that would not support the women's cause condemned Hunt. They would have far preferred a decision they disagreed with to a judicially forced verdict and the dangers that implied. The Rochester *Democrat and Chronicle* called it a "grand overreaching assumption of authority" by a man who believed "he is scarcely lower than the angels so far as personal power goes."

The New York *Sun* attacked Hunt for violating "one of the most important provisions of the Constitution. The right to trial by jury includes the right to a free and impartial verdict." Otherwise the jury would be "twelve wooden automatons, moved by a string pulled by the hand of the judge." The Utica *Observer* approved Hunt's interpretation of the Fourteenth Amendment but nonetheless condemned his seizure of jury power, with which he had "outraged the rights of Susan B. Anthony." The *Legal News* of Chicago charged Hunt with committing a worse offense against the Constitution than Anthony had by "voting illegally," for "he had sworn to support the Constitution and she had not." The Canandaigua *Times* editorialized that despite Anthony's "crime," there is "serious question" of the propriety of a proceeding in which the proper functions of the jury are dispensed with. "If this may be done in one instance, why may it not in all?"

On the morning of the day after the verdict, Selden appealed for a retrial, describing the "jealous care [with which] the right of trial by jury has been guarded by every English speaking people from the days of King John, indeed from the days of King Alfred." He cited a recent New York murder trial which had continued and ended with a conviction even after a juror had become ill. The court of appeals had returned the case for retrial, as "even by a showing of consent" by the defendant, it was not a proper jury. There could never be fewer than twelve people on a true constitutional jury.

Hunt now asked if "the prisoner has anything to say why sentence shall not be pronounced." She replied she had many things to say and began by accusing him of "trampling underfoot every vital principle of our government. I am degraded from the status of citizen to that of a subject [as] all of my sex are by your honor's verdict, doomed to political subjugation under this so-called form of government."

Hunt tried to stop her, but she persisted for some time. Finally, Hunt said, "The court cannot allow the prisoner to go on . . . the prisoner must sit down . . . the court must insist." Anthony sat down after complaining she had "failed even to get a trial by jury not of my peers. I ask not leniency at your hands, but rather the full rigors of the law."

Hunt then fined her one hundred dollars and costs, but she defied him by announcing she would "never pay a dollar of your unjust penalty" but would continue to "rebel against your manmade, unjust, unconstitutional forms of law that tax, fine, imprison and hang women while they deny them the right of representation in the government."

"Madam," Hunt responded, "the court will not order you committed until the fine is paid." His apparent compassion was misleading. By not pressing for payment or imprisoning her, he had avoided criticism for "reversible errors" from higher courts. He had blocked her chance of appeal.

THE CASE AGAINST THE INSPECTORS

The judge was ready to commit more legal offenses in the trial of the three inspectors that afternoon. It was a different jury—again not identified in the record—and Hunt had arranged that they sit through the morning sessions so as to witness his methods.

When the defense attorney John Van Voorhis called one of the supervisors of elections to testify to the advice he had given the inspectors, Hunt ruled the man "incompetent." He did permit Chief Inspector Beverly Jones to testify to the presence of the supervisors Silas J. Wagner, Republican, and Daniel J. Warner, Democrat. Jones went on to report that while Anthony "was reading the Fourteenth Amendment and discussing different points, Mr. Warner said . . ."

Prosecutor Crowley jumped in. "I submit to the court that

it is entirely immaterial what either Warner or Wagner said."

Hunt sustained him, stating, "I don't see that that is competent in any view of the case."

Later Van Voorhis asked Jones to "state what occurred." Again Jones began: "Mr. Warner said . . . ," and again Crowley objected.

Hunt repeated, "I don't think that is competent what Warner said."

"The district attorney has gone into what occurred at that time. I ask to be permitted to show all that occurred."

"I don't think that is competent."

Van Voorhis persisted, demanding that the testimony include what the supervisor said.

"I exclude it."

"Does that exclude all conversations that occurred there with any persons?"

"It excludes anything of that character on the subject of advising them. Your case is just as good without it as with it."

Jones was followed on the stand by his fellow Republican election board member Edwin F. Marsh and other witnesses. One of them was Susan B. Anthony herself, but with all of Crowley's objections sustained by Hunt, she was effectively silenced.

In his summation Van Voorhis stressed the same theme

Many suffragists believed that the Fourteenth and Fifteenth Amendments implicitly gave women the right to vote.

that Selden had in Anthony's defense: malice was essential to crime. "Here is a total absence of any pretense of malice. The defendants acted honestly and according to their best judgment. They are not lawyers, nor skilled in law. They had presented to them a legal question which, to say the least, has puzzled some of the ablest legal minds of the nation."

When he concluded, Crowley rose, but Hunt restrained him. "I don't think it is necessary for you to spend time in argument, Mr. Crowley," he said, and then directed the jury: "Under no circumstance is a woman entitled to vote . . . and by the adjudication which was made this morning upon this subject, there is no discretion. . . . In that view of the case, is there anything to go to the jury?"

Fearing what would come, Van Voorhis jumped up to demand that the "whole case" go to the jury because trial by jury is inviolate and "the court had no power to take it from the jury."

"I am going to submit it to the jury," said Hunt.

"I claim the right to address the jury," said Van Voorhis.

"I don't think there is anything upon which you can legitimately address the jury," Hunt said, and then proceeded to address them himself, stating that the women had no right to offer their votes, nor the inspectors to receive them, but "instead of doing as I did in the case this morning—directing a verdict—I submit the case to you with these instructions, and you can decide it here or go out."

Van Voorhis tried again. "I ask your honor to instruct the jury that if they find these inspectors acted honestly, in accordance with their best judgments, they should be acquitted."

"I have expressly ruled to the contrary of that, gentlemen." Again Hunt charged the jury: "There is sufficient evidence to sustain the indictment upon this point." Van Voorhis asked sarcastically, "Then why should it go to the jury?"

"As a matter of form." Again Hunt tried to force the verdict right there in court. The jurors chose to go out. They returned soon afterward hung, eleven to one for the prosecution. An annoyed Hunt threatened the lone juror: "You may retire again, gentlemen," adding that, unless they agreed within a few minutes, he would adjourn the court until the morning. He did not suggest any food or overnight accommodations for the jurors.

Under this pressure the hesitating juror capitulated, and the panel returned within ten minutes with guilty verdicts for all three defendants. This jury was also quizzed, and again it was clear that it was not the verdict of free choice. Van Voorhis's plea for retrial was dismissed.

Hunt fined the inspectors twenty-five dollars each, but like Anthony they refused to pay, choosing instead to "allow process to be served." Sen. Benjamin Butler of Massachusetts, who had been following the case with great interest, believed that President Grant himself would "remit the fine if they are pressed too far."

And indeed, they were pressed too far. On February 26, 1874, Hunt had the inspectors seized and imprisoned. Anthony rushed to the jail, urged the men to hold out, and promised to work for their early release. She barely rested for five days, lecturing, going to the newspapers, preparing an appeal to Grant for a pardon. On March 2 she returned to the jail with sixty-two dollars for bail and succeeded in having them released.

That same day she received a telegram from Butler saying that Grant had arranged for a pardon and remission of the fines. During their five days in prison the inspectors received hundreds of callers and were served bountiful meals by the women whose votes they had accepted. Upon their release they were widely feted, and when they ran for inspectors at the next election, they were returned to office by a large majority—of male voters.

Anthony was never pardoned because she was never jailed. Judge Selden did appeal to both houses of Congress for remission of her fine, basing his claim on the precedent of publisher Matthew Lyon, who had been imprisoned and fined one thousand dollars after being denied trial by jury under the Alien and Sedition Acts of 1798. That fine was refunded with interest to his heirs. But the reviewing committees in both the Senate and the House rejected the Anthony appeal by narrow margins without considering the chief basis for the claim.

A VIOLATION OF THE CONSTITUTION

In 1897 Van Voorhis remembered the case this way: "There was a pre-arranged determination to convict [Susan B. Anthony]. A jury trial was dangerous, and so the Constitution was openly and deliberately violated.

"The Constitution makes the jury, in criminal cases, the judges of the law and of the facts. The mandate of the Constitution is that no matter how clear or how strong the case may appear to the judge, it must be submitted to the jury," and if the judge controls the jury, "he himself is guilty of a crime for which impeachment is the remedy."

This had been precisely the policy of the Supreme Court since 1794. The first chief justice, John Jay, had written that it is the obligation of the jury to disregard an inequitable law and nullify it. "The jury has a right to judge both law as well as fact in a controversy." The voting trial jurors were, of course, not informed of this.

"If Miss Anthony had won her case on its merits" in the first place, Van Voorhis commented a quarter century after her trial, "it would have revolutionized the suffrage of the country, and enfranchised every woman in the United States."

Consolidating the Suffrage Movement

Ellen Carol DuBois

In the 1880s, Susan B. Anthony began to concentrate on unifying the women's movement behind the cause of suffrage, as Ellen Carol DuBois explains in the following selection from her book *The Elizabeth Cady Stanton–Susan B. Anthony Reader: Correspondence, Writings, Speeches.* A wide variety of women's organizations arose following the Civil War; according to DuBois, Anthony saw even the most conservative of these groups as potential allies and strove to combine them in an umbrella organization dedicated to suffrage. Anthony also played an important role in the 1890 reunification of the conservative and radical wings of the women's rights movement, DuBois maintains. A professor of history and women's studies at the University of California in Los Angeles, DuBois is the author of *Feminism and Suffrage: The Emergence of an Independent Women's Movement in America, 1848–1869.*

The major context for the political role that Elizabeth Cady Stanton and Susan B. Anthony played in the last decades of the nineteenth century was the tremendous expansion in women's reform activities during the 1870s and 1880s. In the years after Reconstruction, middle- and upper-class American women formed and joined an extraordinary number of socially conscious, all-female organizations. These organizations ranged from the innumerable women's clubs that sprang up in every town and city to foster study and sociability, to the larger social reform organizations, especially the Women's Christian Temperance Union (1874), the Young Women's Christian Association (1871), and the Women's Educational and Industrial Union (1877). The dilemma for suffragists was how to relate their concerns for sexual equality and political power to this proliferation of organized public activity among women. Many, like Mary Livermore, Caroline Severance, and Julia Ward Howe, pulled away from the suffrage movement and put their energies into other more popular women's reforms like temperance and pacifism. The response of Stanton and Anthony was different, from this approach and from each other. Anthony tried to unify all organized, reform-minded women around the demand for the vote, whatever their differences over other issues. Stanton, aiming for a more comprehensive political unity, insisted on challenging women whenever she thought they were being too conservative on the wide variety of political issues she believed concerned them.

CHARACTERISTICS OF WOMEN'S GROUPS

In basic ways, the women's organizations of the 1870s and 1880s continued the prewar tradition of women's benevolent and moral reform activity. Their leaders tended to stress women's unique virtues and special responsibility to the community, rather than the identity of men's and women's public roles, which had been the distinguishing argument of women's rights. They placed great emphasis on women's privileged responsibility for domestic life and the rearing of children, and on the moral superiority that they believed flowed from it. Even the religious emphases of prewar women's benevolent activities were maintained in the women's organizations of the period, most of which, despite nominal nonsectarianism and formal independence from church control, were committed to the organization of society around "Christian" values. Traditional "womanly" virtues like self-sacrifice and responsibility for the unfortunate and dependent appeared in a broader light in the context of the rapid industrialization of American society and the social upheaval and human suffering it produced in this period. The responsibility that benevolent women had once felt for pauper widows and orphans they now expressed for the struggling young wage-earning women of the cities. . . .

The relation between these postwar women's organizations and the suffrage movement was complex. The formation of organizations that emphasized the separate spheres of the sexes and the moral superiority of women in their conception of women's public role was both a reaction against and a product of the prominence to which the women's rights perspective had risen in the 1850s and 1860s. On the one hand, many of the leaders of the organizations conceived of them as conservative alternatives to the suffrage movement, and especially to the leadership of Stanton and Anthony. They particularly objected to what they considered excessively radical attacks on femininity and criticisms of the domestic and sexual conventions of bourgeois society. Although there were women's organization leaders who themselves supported the vote, they shared these objections, and believed it was important to create societies where conservative, non-suffrage women could develop and grow. As a result, support for the vote was rarely voiced in postwar women's organizations.

On the other hand, the militant feminism of suffragists changed the traditions of female reform. Unlike prewar societies, most of which were women's auxiliaries, postwar women's organizations were generally free of male control and preached the importance of independence and equality for women. They were assertive about women's capacity to do more than men expected of them and developed techniques for encouraging women to gain wider interests and new skills. Perhaps most important, they no longer insisted that women's influence be limited to the domestic circle and did not consider public life exclusively masculine. Most of these organizations moved over time in the direction of political activity. The WCTU, for instance, soon abandoned prayer to advocate anti-liquor laws, and women's clubs concentrated on programs of municipal reform. The fear of overstepping "woman's sphere," which had restrained women's reform organizations before the rise of the women's rights movement, had largely faded, and women were beginning to recognize the necessity of political action, which was a basic premise of suffragism.

Initially, Anthony was not very enthusiastic about the postwar proliferation of women's organizations and reform activities. It was a cardinal article of faith for her that any work which did not focus on enfranchisement was fruitless for women to pursue. Gradually, however, she began to recognize that there was a great deal of pro-suffrage sentiment latent in the non-suffrage women's organizations. In this regard, the achievements of Frances Willard in the WCTU especially impressed her. Initially, the leaders of the WCTU had been explicitly opposed to woman suffrage. Willard, who was elected second president of the WCTU in 1879, was a suffragist. In 1881, she risked her presidency to advocate full political equality for women, and won the support of most of the members. By the 1890s, WCTU women constituted the majority of suffrage activists in the West and Midwest. Willard's successes demonstrated that support for the suffrage could be made compatible with relatively conventional ideas about the role of women and that it was therefore possible to create a much larger and broader woman suffrage movement than had been built before.

WORKING FOR A BROAD CONSENSUS

With the example of Willard behind her, Anthony began to work toward the formation of a broad consensus in favor of woman suffrage among all organized, reform-minded women. In order to achieve this goal Anthony was willing to accommodate herself to, rather than to challenge, the conservative beliefs about women and the family that flourished among such women. She had to retreat from the various radicalisms with which her leadership of the suffrage movement had long been associated. "Our intention . . . is [simply] to make every one . . . believe in the grand principle of equality of rights and chances for women . . . ," she wrote, in 1884, in an effort to keep Stanton from raising a controversial issue at a suffrage convention. "Neither you nor I have the right . . . to complicate or compromise our question." Anthony even had to abandon the tactical militancy, for which she had always had a strong personal attraction, because it was "unladylike" and offended women who accepted the rule of respectability. Instead of a movement of women united around an explicit political program for the transformation of society and women's place in it, she began to envision the unification of all women, whatever their social or political beliefs, around their common womanhood and the single goal of political equality. Beginning in the mid–1880s, Anthony began to dedicate her considerable energies and powers of organization to the consolidation of the many postwar women's reform organizations into a single, unified "woman movement."

Under Anthony's leadership, suffragists took on the work of unifying the various women's organizations. . . .

A permanent National Council of Women was formed in

1888, the first multi-reform national women's organization ever founded in the United States; its goals included equal pay for women, increased access to industrial and professional education, and a single moral standard for both sexes. The formation of the National Council of Women was followed within a year by the creation of a second national organization, the General Federation of Women's Clubs. Both the National Council and the General Federation encouraged the formation of state and local affiliates and did a great deal to increase and consolidate women's ability to control community institutions and affect state and municipal governments.

However, these developments did not generate as much support for woman suffrage as Anthony had hoped they would. . . . The National Council of Women refused to adopt woman suffrage as one of its principles. . . . Nor did the General Federation of Women's Clubs support suffrage until 1914, on the very eve of victory. Anthony was mystified and disappointed by the fact that the consolidation of American women's organizations, to which she had contributed so much, had not done more to benefit woman suffrage. "The Federation of Clubs . . . can count forty thousand members . . . the Christian Temperance Union . . . can report a half-million members; I will tell you frankly and honestly that all we number is seven thousand," she explained in 1893. ". . . what a hindrance this lack has been. . . . If we could have demonstrated to the Congress . . . that we had a thorough organization back of our demand, we should have had all our demands granted long ago."

REUNIFICATION

Simultaneous with the Council, and out of a similar spirit of harmony and the desire to draw together women's organizational power, the suffrage movement itself begin to unite. Ever since the initial split in 1869 there had been many calls for the unification of the National Woman Suffrage Association, led by Stanton and Anthony, and the American Woman Suffrage Association, led by Lucy Stone and Henry Blackwell, but not until the late 1880s were there any initiatives from the leaders of either organization. In 1887, Alice Stone Blackwell, daughter of Stone and Blackwell and corresponding secretary of the American, proposed a joint meeting to consider merger. In a later account of the period, she explained that the American became willing to merge with the National because "the question of easy divorce" and "persons . . . of notorious immorality" were no longer welcomed on the National's platform. Representatives of the National responded enthusiastically to her invitation, formed a committee to discuss unification, and invited the leaders of the American to participate in the 1888 International Council of Women, which was the first time the two organizations had cooperated in many years.

Within the National, Anthony was a leading force for merger. From the beginning of the negotiations process, she was convinced that "the best good for women's enfranchisement . . . surely will come through the union of all the friends of woman suffrage into one great and grand National Association. . . ." Her enthusiasm was consistent with her general effort in this period to set aside political differences among women in order to create the largest possible unity around the demand for the vote. At no time during the negotiations did she question the desirability of the merger or seriously examine the terms in which it was being proposed. "I cannot think of any stipulation I wish to make the basis of union," she wrote, "save that we unite and after that discuss all measures. . . ." Her position surprised many in light of the intense hatred she had often expressed for the leaders of the American, especially for Lucy Stone. To herself and others, Anthony justified her reversal by contending that the American was anxious to affiliate with the National, which it now recognized as the stronger and more successful of the two organizations. "They have always been on the *defensive* . . . ," she wrote to Olympia Brown, ". . . while we have gone on from triumph to triumph, until they see and feel and want to share our glory and power." Inasmuch as most of the terms of the merger were set by the American, there was considerable self-deception involved in her claim that the American was dissolving itself into the National.

Despite Anthony's authority and her efforts to convince friends and recruits to "stand by Susan once more," she faced opposition within the National that delayed the merger for two years. Leading opponents to the move included veteran suffragists like Olympia Brown and Matilda Joslyn Gage, and young activists such as Clara Colby and Harriette Shattuck. Linking all their objections was their fear that the essence of the National's approach to suffrage would somehow be lost through unification. They were concerned that merger would lead to the abandonment of the National's strategic focus on federal citizenship and the ideological message it carried of women's full and absolute equality with men. They feared that suffragists would concentrate instead on enfranchisement at the state level, or worse, on partial suffrages, like the school or municipal vote. They objected to the proposed plan of organization, which they charged would shift the focus of organizational activity from the national society to the state and local affiliates. Opponents of the merger believed that a majority of the members of the National supported them, and moved that the issue be submitted to a vote of the whole organization, but the National's Executive Committee, which was controlled by pro-union forces, refused, and itself made the decision to merge with the American. "The executive sessions . . . were the most stormy in the history of the association," Ida Harper, Anthony's biographer, wrote, "and only the unsurpassed parliamentary knowledge of the chairman, May Wright Sewall, aided by the firm cooperation of Miss Anthony, could have harmonized the opposing elements and secured a majority in favor of union." In February, 1890, the two organizations met in joint convention and declared themselves the National American Woman Suffrage Association (NAWSA).

The unification of the suffrage movement reflected the belief that political and ideological differences among women were far less important than, and could be subordinated to, their common struggle for enfranchisement. "The time is past when the mass of the suffrage women will be compromised by any one person's peculiarities!" Anthony wrote Stanton in 1897. "We number over ten thousand women and each one has opinions . . . and we can only hold them together to work for the ballot by letting alone their whims and prejudices on other subjects." Thus, although Anthony was personally antiracist, she opposed all efforts to raise the question of discrimination against Black women in the NAWSA because she feared it would anger Southern white suffragists. This approach to unity within the feminist movement was paralleled by a strategy for winning support outside it that refused to make political distinctions among potential allies. This "nonpartisan" approach was explicitly articulated at the NAWSA's founding convention, during a session on "Our Attitude Toward Political Parties." "The sentiment was in favor of keeping strictly aloof from all political alliances," Anthony and Ida Harper wrote. "It was shown that suffrage can only be gained through the assistance of men in all parties." The "nonpartisan" posture that Anthony helped to shape remained the official strategy of the NAWSA for the next thirty years, and was carried over, after the vote was won, into the NAWSA's successor, the League of Women Voters.

THE DRAWBACKS OF THE "NONPARTISAN" POLICY

However, the strategy of nonpartisanship had its weaknesses. It put a great deal of pressure on suffragists not to do anything that would divide their movement or drive support away. The result was a suffrage organization that could not tolerate serious political dissent and forced it outside. Throughout its history, the NAWSA was plagued by a series of organizational secessions, beginning with the Women's National Liberation Association, formed by Matilda Gage in 1890, and culminating in the Congressional Union, which broke away from the NAWSA in 1913. Moreover, nonpartisanship was at crucial points an illusion. Even while the NAWSA proclaimed that it held aloof from politics, its "nonpartisan" stance both encouraged and helped to obscure the conservative ideas that were coming to dominate it, not only about women's role but about social reform in general. The NAWSA's antiradical bias began to emerge in reaction to the growth of Populism in the 1890s. In South Dakota, Kansas, and other states where Populists instigated and led woman suffrage campaigns, Anthony and other NAWSA leaders, barely hiding their distaste for Populist radicalism, concentrated their energies on courting Republican support, and organized "nonpartisan" suffrage societies in which only Republican women participated. Some political conflicts are impossible to avoid, and in these cases the NAWSA's "nonpartisanship" inclined it toward conservatism and away from those who challenged established power, encouraged conflict, and exposed and mobilized social discontent.

The Beginnings of an International Movement for Women's Rights

Mildred Adams

Susan B. Anthony took her first trip to England and Europe in 1883. While there, she met with influential women of several countries and was introduced to the leaders of the fledgling British suffrage movement. As author Mildred Adams relates in the following passage from her book *The Right to Be People*, these experiences led Anthony to consider expanding the women's rights movement beyond the United States. Adams examines her efforts to form an international organization, which culminated in the first meeting of the International Council of Women in Washington, D.C., in 1888, attended by representatives of forty-nine nations.

The century was moving on, new forces were emerging, famous suffragists were growing older. Elizabeth Cady Stanton retired as a professional public speaker in 1880. Limited suffrage was granted to women in Kansas, Michigan, and Minnesota; by 1890 there were nineteen states that had given women local school suffrage. These piecemeal victories were more important as indicating a slow shift in public opinion than as promising full suffrage. . . .

The national scene within which the suffragists moved was changing. The country continued to grow, and to grow together. Many people moved westward, a few of them moved south. Transportation improved; so did communication. Boston, which in the 1840's had seemed self-sufficient, superior, far from New York, was now recognizing the growing importance of Washington, and could even contemplate Chicago.

Susan B. Anthony, somewhat to her surprise, came to contemplate Europe.

The circumstances of her first trip abroad say much for the inner warmth of this spare, stern suffragist. Despite her somewhat forbidding exterior (an exterior that lent itself all too well to the skill of cartoonists) she had gained with the years so deep a belief in the moral rightness of her cause that it shone on her plain face and drew to her women of courage and discernment. Our Susan was too downright to be called a saint, and too emphatic of tongue, but as she grew older she developed an inward grace, an illumination of countenance that attracted both the young and the experienced. Also, she was acquiring the attraction that attaches to fame.

An Excuse to Travel

In Philadelphia, at the end of the seventies, she met two young women, Rachel and Julia Foster, daughters of a liberal Pittsburgh editor who, at his death two years earlier, had left his wife and children dowered with a comfortable fortune. Rachel, restless and curious, feeling herself modern in the terms of those days, took an immediate liking to the old reformer, joined her workers and planned some lecture tours for her. The two became warm friends. When Mrs. Stanton, who had gone abroad on a holiday, wrote urging Susan to join her, Rachel Foster discovered excellent reasons to second the invitation. She had always wanted to go to Europe, but being a young lady of good family she could not go unaccompanied. What better idea than to persuade Susan to go with her as chaperone and traveling companion?

Left to herself, it is doubtful that Susan would have broken her old habits and embarked on an adventure that must have seemed extravagant in time as well as money. But the Fosters were offering to meet traveling expenses, Susan was dog-tired, and she had the prospect of a long-promised bequest that would enable her to go straight back to suffrage lecturing when she got home. . . .

By this time Susan had become a famous character in many places. People with other convictions still disagreed with her crusade, but something about the selfless and indomitable nature of crusade and crusader caught their respect. When, in the winter of 1883, it became known that she would be traveling abroad there was a wide stirring of interest, and even editorials praising her as a representative American who would be honored in Europe. A hundred dollars came in as a gift from an anonymous friend, receptions were given, and speeches made. Susan responded with the characteristic hope that "while abroad I shall do something to recommend our work here, so as to make them [the Europeans] respect American women and their demand for political equality."

The trip was planned primarily for the education of the young and well-born Miss Foster, but it also fitted the wishes of the older traveler. Susan was determined to get all she could out of what she assumed would be her only foreign trip. She read guidebooks, she made notes in her diary. In February of 1883 the two women headed out across the cold Atlantic (a "beaver-lined satin circular" was Miss Anthony's provision against the weather) and spent a week with Mrs. Stanton in London. She went to Rome, to Switzerland, to Paris. In Paris, Rachel left her for a short time in the home of a hospitable friend of women's rights whose English was as scarce as Susan's French. There, for the first time in her hard-working life, Susan "positively ate my breakfast in bed. What my dear mother would pronounce most lazily."

When, after this mild debauch, she got back to England, it was to plunge into suffrage affairs on another level. By 1883 the English women, whose long campaign for the vote had been started in 1866 by a petition introduced into Parliament by John Stuart Mill, had acquired the vote in municipal elections as well as some property rights. The suffrage movement, however, was split into several parts. Susan found herself welcomed and courted by invitations from many quarters. Even her wardrobe, which she had thought ample, began to seem inadequate and she ordered "a dark garnet velvet dress at Waterloo House." Regarded as an obvious extravagance, it was to serve her as her proudest garment on platforms and receptions for years to come.

Her last point of call was Ireland, to which she was pulled in part by her gratitude to George Train, who had started her career as editor with *The Revolution.* Even though he had left her with promises that were never fulfilled, and that $10,000 debt to pay off at the end, she had never forgotten the lift that his support gave her after the 1866 Kansas suffrage referendum defeat. In addition to this was a desire to see for herself the home circumstances that thousands of Irish girls, ignorant but determined not to starve, had left to emigrate to domestic jobs in the United States.

What she saw appalled her. Poverty in Ireland in 1883 was neither attractive, romantic, or forgivable. The visible state of the Irish poor so shocked and distressed her that for the first time in her life she failed to complete her schedule and fled from a situation she could not help.

Susan returned to England in October and waited there a month for Mrs. Stanton whose daughter, married to an Englishman, was about to give birth. On the eve of departure from Liverpool she persuaded herself to take a step into the international field that had been in her mind ever since she left the United States. She felt that somehow a link should be established between the suffrage forces at home and those in England. Daunted by the bitter divisions she had found between the English groups, she had withheld her hand. Now she was about to leave; unless she acted at once she must go home with a sense of failure. Braced by Mrs. Stanton's enthusiasm, she proposed to the small group of Liverpool suffragists (reinforced by London friends who had come to see her off) that they form then and there an international committee for women's rights. This proved to be the start of a movement that would circle the globe. The International Council of Women with members in fifty-eight countries would grow from this small seed.

THE FIRST INTERNATIONAL MEETING

It took five years for the seed to put up a sizable shoot; Susan kept it alive by correspondence with the committee that she and Mrs. Stanton had set up in Liverpool, and by constant mention of it in suffrage conventions in the United States. By 1887 she was able to persuade the National Woman Suffrage Association to sponsor in Washington a meeting of the International Council of Women. It was to be held in 1888, to celebrate the fortieth anniversary of the Declaration of Women's Rights, and to "give women a realizing sense of the power of combination." Suffrage was to be only one of many subjects discussed. It was the subject nearest Susan's heart, but she had become more and more a realist. Remembering from her travels in Europe how little support woman suffrage had on the continent, and how divided the English women were, she recognized that if she gave her desire for the vote too much prominence in Washington, she might alienate some of the visitors she most valued. To get them to come, and then to persuade them of the importance of her cause—that was the strategy.

The International Council met with flags, speeches, and a more substantial public success than its best wishers could have expected. Albaugh's opera house, famous in 1888 as the largest public meeting place in Washington, was crowded for eight afternoons and evenings. Forty-nine nations were represented, and fifty-three American organizations. Among the latter was the American Woman Suffrage Association of the Boston ladies estranged for years from the National, but yielding to the drawing power of those forty-nine foreign states. Representing it were Susan's well-known and now elderly rivals, Lucy Stone and her husband Henry Blackwell, Julia Ward Howe, Mary Livermore. They all had honored places on the program, they all made speeches. . . .

The International Council of Women was at that meeting made a permanent organization. Its meetings would take Susan to Europe again and again, until her somewhat hazy dream in 1883 of alerting the world to women's protests against repression and women's demands for the vote would take form and force.

Anthony's Work for Coeducation

Zoë Ingalls

One of the issues that concerned the women's rights movement was coeducation. Most colleges and universities—both public and private—were closed to women, including some of the most prestigious schools in the nation. Susan B. Anthony and other feminists worked hard to convince these schools to admit qualified young women as students. One of the most exhaustive battles occurred in Anthony's own hometown of Rochester, New York. In the following article, Zoë Ingalls describes Anthony's efforts to open the University of Rochester to female students, including a last-minute fund-raising drive in which Anthony accomplished the seemingly impossible. Ingalls is a U.S. correspondent for the *Chronicle of Higher Education.*

All through the summer, Vera Chadsey waited anxiously for the outcome of an unusual fund-raising effort. If the citizens of Rochester, New York, could raise $50,000 by September 8, 1900, the University of Rochester would admit women as undergraduates for the first time in its 50-year history.

Miss Chadsey, who had just graduated from high school, hoped to be in the first class. "My father said if they succeeded, I could go," she wrote in a letter of reminiscence in 1960. It was the only path to higher education open to her; her family could not afford to send her away to a women's college.

"It will be very hard for any of the women and girls now to realize the prejudice [against] higher education for girls at that time," she wrote. "The great middle class considered a high school education plenty for any girl."

All that summer, she alternated between excitement and pessimism. "It would come over me that it was only a fairy tale, it could not really happen to me," she wrote.

Women were, indeed, admitted to the University of Rochester. The year 2000 marks the 100th anniversary of co-education there, as well as the 150th anniversary of the university's founding. . . .

ANTHONY'S ROLE

The story of how Vera Chadsey and 32 other young women came to be admitted 100 years ago is little known outside this city, even though Susan B. Anthony, one of its most famous residents, played a major role. It is a story of courage, perseverance, and an 11th-hour rescue worthy of any cliffhanger.

Many of its details are available in the special-collections archive of the university's library, a few miles from the red-brick house where Anthony lived for 40 years. The archive holds several important collections related to Anthony, comprising letters, photographs, newspaper clippings, memorabilia, and artifacts like her handkerchief, dress buttons, and her cup and saucer.

The library also has Vera Chadsey's original 1960 letter, typed on white notepaper and signed with her married name, Twichell. Mary M. Huth, the university's assistant head of rare books and special collections, handles the sheet with reverence. "When I first read that Twichell letter, I think it made it much more obvious what coeducation meant to this young woman," she says. "I knew the university had been opened to women, but not what a life-changing thing it was for her."

Vera Chadsey Twichell's letter reveals a personal reaction to the event; other items in the collections, including the minutes of the university's Board of Trustees, fill in many of the historical details.

The story begins, of course, with the growth of demands for women's rights. Anthony believed that suffrage and education were "where the focus of women's organizing energies should be," says Nora Bredes, director of the university's Susan B. Anthony Center for Women's Leadership.

Anthony "felt that to break open those two areas would give women the tools they needed to do everything else."

In 1893, Anthony paid for a young woman named Helen Wilkinson to take a full load of courses at the university, although she could not matriculate. Miss Wilkinson withdrew because of ill health after attending classes for two years, and died two years later. Anthony put the young woman's portrait in her house, and it can be seen there today, in the hall outside Anthony's second-floor bedroom.

Anthony and others continued to push hard for the admission of women, but they met with stubborn opposition from many alumni. On June 14, 1898, however, there was a breakthrough. The university's trustees agreed to admit women "upon the same terms and under the same conditions as men"—provided that the proponents of coeducation raise $100,000 to pay for the capital improvements and other expenditures that would be necessary. That sum is the equivalent of nearly $2-million today.

A committee of prominent women was formed to raise the funds. But on June 12, 1900, after two years of efforts, they dolefully reported to the trustees that they had raised just $40,000 and were likely to raise only $10,000 more.

The trustees, after a heated discussion, softened their terms. They agreed to admit women in September of that year, "provided that $50,000 is secured in good subscriptions by that time." The deadline was Saturday, September 8, the date of the next meeting of the board's executive committee.

Anthony, believing that the fund-raising effort was in capable hands, embarked on a lecture tour in the West. She returned, exhausted, just a few days before the deadline set by the board. (She was, after all, 80 years old at the time.)

DOWN TO THE WIRE

The night before the board was to meet, Anthony received a call from Fannie Bigelow, treasurer of the committee, who reported that it was still $8,000 short of the amount needed, and that the trustees were unlikely to extend the deadline.

Anthony "went to bed to pass a sleepless night, turning over and over in her mind every possibility for getting that $8,000," wrote her contemporaneous biographer, Ida Husted Harper. The next morning, Anthony spoke with her sister, Mary Anthony, who had planned to give $2,000 to the university when it accepted women. "Give it now," Anthony said, "or the girls may never be admitted." Her sister agreed.

Then Anthony put on her bonnet, climbed into her carriage and began calling on potential donors. By midafternoon, she had succeeded in raising $4,000 more—but the total was still $2,000 short. The board was already in session, and Anthony feared that it would adjourn before she could show up. Finally, securing the last $2,000 from her friend Samuel Wilder, she sped to the building where the trustees had gathered.

According to the minutes of that meeting, the men were discussing a request to increase an instructor's salary by $1,200 when Anthony, like a deus ex machina in black silk, entered with her companions.

"Her voice shaking with excitement, Miss Anthony laid before them the pledges for the remaining $8,000," wrote Harper.

But it still wasn't over. The trustees refused to accept the $2,000 from Mr. Wilder, who was in ill health; if he died, they reasoned, his estate might not honor the pledge.

Anthony was stunned, but she quickly recovered. Rising from her chair and walking to the table where the trustees sat, she told them that she would pledge her own life-insurance policy, worth $2,000, to make up the difference.

"They let the girls in," Anthony later wrote in her diary. "[T]here was no alternative."

Two days later, Anthony collapsed from a stroke. Although she lived for six more years, she was never to enjoy full health again, says Ms. Bredes, director of the women's-leadership center.

PAYING HOMAGE

The university has acknowledged Anthony's contributions in a variety of ways over the years. In addition to the leadership center, which works for "women's full social, political, and economic equality," there is the Susan B. Anthony Institute for Gender and Women's Studies, and a dormitory, a scholarship, and an undergraduate prize in her name.

One of the high points of the centennial celebration is the first Susan B. Anthony Legacy Race, a 5-kilometer run from Anthony's house to the university's River Campus. The race, held in September 2000, commemorates "the last-minute push to raise the funds necessary to get women into the university" says Ms. Bredes. The runners carried Susan B. Anthony dollar coins, which were collected at the finish line to be donated to the scholarship fund that bears her name.

Ms. Bredes sees the race as a way to remind "younger women and men" of "the urgency, the commitment Anthony felt."

Most young women today don't appreciate fully what Anthony did for them, Ms. Bredes adds. "It's part of our job to make women understand what she won, and how dear it was."

For that, she might refer them to the letter of Vera Chadsey Twichell, University of Rochester, Class of 1904. "I wish I could make you girls and women of today realize what going to college meant to me and to many other girls also," she wrote.

"To actually go to college, and really graduate, and wear a cap and gown, the very thought of it made every nerve in my body tingle."

Anthony's Oratorical Skills

Kathleen Barry

Kathleen Barry is a professor of human development and sociology at Pennsylvania State University. Her books include *Susan B. Anthony: A Biography of a Singular Feminist.* In the following essay, Barry examines Anthony's skills as a lecturer and as the international spokesperson for women's rights. She traces Anthony's development as an orator through her early years of working the lecture circuit to her last public speech at the age of eighty-six. In addition, Barry explores some of Anthony's primary theories about women's status and their rights in the context of her speeches.

Susan B. Anthony's public career as a spokeswoman for and leader of the woman's rights movement spanned fifty-six years—the entire second half of the nineteenth century into the early years of the twentieth. During that time, she witnessed small gains for women, such as slowly evolving access to higher education, and large losses, such as repeated defeats of constitutional amendments granting women suffrage. In the 1840s, her early career as a school teacher eventually led her into public speaking on temperance issues. In the early 1850s, she discovered her talent for arousing women to action in their own behalf as she built organizational structures from local societies to state and national associations. She increased opportunities for women to speak in public by organizing national woman's rights conventions and petition campaigns throughout the 1850s, even after many women activists had returned to their family responsibilities.

By the time of her arrest in 1872 for voting, Anthony had gained recognition as the charismatic leader of efforts for woman's rights. By the 1880s, she had taken her campaigns

From *Women Public Speakers in the United States, 1800–1925: A Bio-Critical Sourcebook*, edited by Karlyn Kohrs Campbell. Copyright © 1993 by Karlyn Kohrs Campbell. Reproduced with permission of Greenwood Publishing Group, Inc., Westport, CT.

to Europe and laid the foundation for an international movement. From then until her death in 1906, in both her organizing efforts and her lectures, her focus was on women's
political power through suffrage. Recognized for giving her
life to the cause of women's emancipation, by the turn of the
century she had become the international spokesperson of
woman's rights. . . .

EARLY SPEECHES

Anthony's work placed her before the public more than any
other woman at that time. She conducted conventions, made
appeals to legislatures, and traveled the lecture circuits for
months at a time each year. Without particular connection to
the reform aristocracy and without the class privilege that
brings with it entitlement, she rose to become a national and
then an international leader of woman's rights. Her persua-
siveness on the lecture circuit was due in significant part to
her similarities to the women in remote villages whose interests she championed. Her early life had typified the ordi-
nariness and economic meagerness of the lives of the girls
and women of her time. Women saw in her the common
woman of their own lives.

In her formative years, Anthony had been inculcated
with the traditional ideology of True Womanhood of her
time, which she adopted with special fervor in early adulthood. As a young woman, still years away from the public
platform, she was selectively fervent about the moralistic
piety that defined True Womanhood, choosing to ignore its
intention to keep women in their assigned private sphere.
Her early temperance lectures reveal some of the moralistic piety and righteousness that she eventually transformed
into political consciousness and a civil, publicly responsible
morality. From the beginning, hers was a search to find and
challenge the root cause of women's suffering and their inferior status. She began with the woman abuse that came
from men's intemperance:

> We would that some means were devised, by which our
> Brothers and sons shall no longer be allured from the *right*
> by the corrupting influences of the fashionable sippings of
> wine and brandy, those sure destroyers of Mental and Moral
> Worth, and by which our Sisters and daughters shall no
> longer be exposed to the vile arts of the gentlemanly appear-
> ing gallant, but really half-inebriated seducers.

In this speech, Anthony was searching for "plans which

may produce a radical change in our Moral Atmosphere," but her words had not yet matched the actual roots of women's subordination. Lecturing fed her developing political consciousness because it connected her to women's daily lives. In turn, she converted her new knowledge into political consciousness. On the lecture circuit, speaking in villages throughout New York State in the early 1850s, she discovered the limitations of her temperance campaigns. She talked with women in their kitchens and saw the actual conditions of their lives. She left behind the old morality of True Womanhood and turned her intense energy toward initiating lecture campaigns and petition drives to secure married women property rights in an age when marriage suspended women's legal existence and, thus, their rights to inherit, own property, conduct their own businesses, or even share custody of their own children. Petitioning was a means to tie the woman's rights messages of her lectures to political action that involved her audiences.

However great Anthony's ties were to common women, by the mid-1850s she herself was rising to national prominence. Few women sustained full careers as public orators at this time. Furthermore, she was neither a wife nor an "old maid," neither comfortably middle-class nor poor; she supported herself solely on the little money she earned from lecturing. At this time she and Elizabeth Cady Stanton met. Their lifelong friendship and deep, loving commitment to each other provided Anthony with a peer—a true equal—in friendship and politics. This friendship would sustain her through her long tours of duty on the lecture circuit. . . .

The 1850s was the woman's rights decade of radicalism and political consciousness in which speeches produced by Anthony and Cady Stanton together, along with their separate statements, became the foundation of the politics and philosophy of their movement. Together they penned "On Educating the Sexes Together," a speech that Anthony delivered in New York and Massachusetts in 1856. It bore the strong influence of Cady Stanton's analysis of natural rights. In demanding coeducation, they reasoned that if

> it would be ridiculous to talk of male and female atmospheres, male & female rains, male & female sunshine, or male & female elements in any part of nature, how much more ridiculous is it in relation to mind, to soul, to thought, where there is as undeniably no such thing as sex, to talk of male & female education & male and female schools.

Anthony's own politics were less shaped by studied philosophies and movement ideologies than were Cady Stanton's, nor did her own rhetoric reflect them. In expounding her views, Anthony drew from pieces and patches at hand, the way she had in making quilts when she was growing up at home. Natural rights became mixed with some Quaker egalitarianism, fired by some of her father's temperance convictions—all of which took on a new, different meaning when she developed them into her own woman's rights rhetoric.

As Anthony cultivated her own ideas and direction for her woman's rights work, her rhetoric became focused on her belief in the unlimited human potential for progress, development, and growth, a key theme of liberalism and its ideas of progress. She fitted these ideas into a conception of woman's enlightenment that was neither natural rights philosophy nor the ideology of liberalism. It was a new, vital woman-oriented consciousness that shaped philosophy as it emerged in political action. The foundation of Anthony's politics, her speeches, and her organizing was her belief in human immortality. "There is indwelling in every human being irrespective of color, or sex, or condition, the indestructible, though perchance from unfortunate circumstances of birth and surroundings, scarcely recognizable germ of immutable life, susceptible of unlimited culture, growth and development." This belief in something spiritual that could not be destroyed even by all the oppression she saw around her motivated her to work, campaign, and struggle through defeats and sometimes seemingly insurmountable odds. What the idea of progress had given to the theme of the common man, which encouraged men to move upward and outward in society, Anthony articulated to create a utopian vision for women. She formulated this dream in her 1857 speech "The True Woman," which gives much of the basis of her politics and thinking. To incorporate women into the idea of progress, she developed an egalitarian image of a new true woman:

> The true woman will not be exponent of another, or allow another to be such for her. She will be her own individual self,—do her own individual work,—stand or fall by her own individual wisdom and strength. . . . She will proclaim the "glad tidings of good news" to all women, that woman equally with man was made for her own individual happiness, to develop every power of her three-fold nature, to use, worthily, every

talent given her by God, in the great work of life, to the best advantage of herself and the race.

AN OPTIMISTIC VISIONARY

. . . By the mid–1850s, Anthony was in as much demand on the anti-slavery circuit as she was on woman's rights. . . . Her speeches were optimistic and visionary. More important, they were solidly lodged in her belief in the inviolability and immortality of the human being. That belief was the foundation for her lifetime commitment to the universality of rights and equality. Her rhetoric centered on the integrity and potential of the human being, which made her egalitarianism universal whether she was discussing marriage, slavery, working women, or suffrage. . . .

The same tough-minded, unswerving egalitarianism that attracted abolitionists to her in the 1850s turned them away in the 1860s when it was clear that her standards were universal: she would not subordinate woman's rights to any other cause. The radicalism of Anthony and Cady Stanton, reaching as it did to the roots of women's subordination in marriage, caused reformers, especially the abolitionists, to turn against them. Anthony was undaunted. When William Lloyd Garrison told her she should not offer refuge to an abused wife of a prominent politician, she relied on analogy to convey the universality of her politics:

> That I should stop to ask if my act would injure the reputation of any movement never crossed my mind, nor will I now allow such a fear to stifle my sympathies or tempt me to expose her to the cruel, inhuman treatment of her own household. Trust me that as I ignore all law to help the slave, so will I ignore it all to protect the enslaved woman.

This letter to Garrison reveals the conformity of Anthony's public rhetoric and action to her private correspondence. For her there was no difference in the two worlds. Her universal approach to rights became the basis of her singular commitment to championing woman's rights when the abolitionists rejected universal suffrage. . . .

PRACTICAL AND PLAIN

By 1870, Susan B. Anthony had become a charismatic leader. By this time, it was known that her life was the cause of women; that she withstood the rigors of demanding daily lectures for months at a time, staying in the field long after others left to recuperate; that she lived frugally, allowing herself one new dress a year, always a black one so the gaiety of colors and prints that she loved would not detract from her message.

DEDUCTIVE LOGIC IN ANTHONY'S SPEECHES

Susan B. Anthony employed logical argumentation in her suffrage speeches, writes Allen H. Merriam, a professor of communications at Missouri Southern State College in Joplin. In the following passage, Merriam lists various rhetorical devices that Anthony used to bolster her reasoning and persuade her audiences.

Anthony's suffrage speeches reflected a strong reliance on logical argumentation. Her reasoning was primarily deductive, emanating from general principles such as that discrimination is wrong, that the denial of political rights destroys economic and moral well-being, and that individual freedom is a natural right. Her evidence took many forms: statistics ("In New York alone, there are over 50,000 . . . women receiving less than fifty cents a day"); quotations ("Alexander Hamilton said one hundred years ago, 'Give to a man the right over my subsistence, and he has power over my whole moral being'"); comparisons (often of the plight of women to the degradation of blacks under slavery); and historical allusions appealing to patriotic emotions ("With man, woman shared the dangers of the Mayflower on a stormy sea, the dreary landing on Plymouth Rock, the rigors of New England winters, and the privations of a seven years' war"). Anthony relied heavily on quotations from the Declaration of Independence and the U.S. Constitution to establish the legal basis for political liberties.

Allen H. Merriam, "Susan B. Anthony (1820–1906), Suffragist," in *American Orators Before 1900: Critical Studies and Sources,* ed. Bernard K. Duffy and Halford R. Ryan, 1987.

By 1870, when she realized that without political power women would not be able to achieve and secure equal status, Anthony focused on suffrage in her speeches but always connected it to the wide range of women's issues. She had come to see denial of suffrage as the root cause of women's secondary status because it denied women the political power to shape their destinies. In her speeches Anthony enumerated the arguments raised by opponents of woman's rights—that men supported women so they did not need to support themselves, that work degraded women. Then she marshalled facts to answer these arguments, bringing all the issues to bear on woman's political disfranchisement. She always fitted her examples to her particular audience (working women, married women, teachers). In each speech she made a specific appeal to the men who, as she knew, held the family purse and the right to vote for woman suffrage. Her strategy was to ask them to take the higher road and not debase themselves to the condition of slave master as other men were doing in examples she gave.

Anthony's speeches were unadorned with the evangelical flourishes typical of that period. "I come tonight neither as an orator nor a philosopher, but as a representative of the working women," began one of her many logical, pragmatic lectures (*San Francisco Evening Bulletin*, July 13, 1871). She never considered herself a good speaker, and many of her long, handwritten speeches are laborious to read. But their oral delivery, fortified with her passion, gave them added power. . . .

Anthony's persuasive powers were strongest when she spoke extemporaneously. In her public appearances, she always dressed in loosely fitting clothes to prevent any confinement when she was on the public platform. At her 1873 trial for voting, these elements combined with her charismatic appeal to produce one of her finest and most enduring rhetorical works. After she sat through the mockery of a trial and heard the federal judge direct the jury to bring in a verdict that she was guilty of having voted in the national elections of 1872, the judge asked, "Has the prisoner anything to say why sentence shall not be pronounced?" In court she had been caught by surprise when the judge refused to turn the case over to the jury, but now she spoke her mind without notes or written statements. . . .

The essence of Anthony's charismatic message was her indignation and her refusal to recognize a court, laws, or a country that violated her (and all women's) rights. She would not acknowledge or concede to being a subject to unjust rule. She ignored rebukes from the judge that he would not tolerate her speech, and she also ignored his orders to sit down and be silent. . . .

WORKING THE LECTURE CIRCUIT

Anthony had been the publisher of the *Revolution*, a radical feminist newspaper, from 1868 to 1870, and when it failed, she was forced to work the lecture circuit for six years to pay off the $10,000 debt. When that was paid, she began work on financing the *History of Woman Suffrage*, as well as financing one suffrage campaign after another, which kept her full time on the lecture circuit to support the movement and herself.

By the 1880s, Anthony had become conscious that in championing woman's rights, she and her movement were not only making history but were also creating a historical legacy for future generations. She was determined that women would write their own history. With Cady Stanton and Matilda Joslyn Gage, she produced and published three volumes of the *History of Woman Suffrage*. She produced a fourth volume with Ida Harper, who also wrote the three-volume *Life and Work of Susan B. Anthony* that she insisted be written as she came to realize that her own life had also become a history of the movement.

Through her travels to Europe in the 1880s, Anthony generated an international woman's movement. Although she organized its first meeting in 1888, it was not until 1902, four years before her death at age eighty-six, that she saw the International Council of Women unite in the struggle for suffrage. She considered this accomplishment the climax of her career. To the end of her life universal rights and a pragmatic approach to political action marked her approach to her public work, which had become synonymous with her private life. In the 1890s, she refused to support racist and class-based proposals for educated suffrage, which would exclude the poor, most immigrants, and African-Americans. When considering who was qualified to vote, she argued for an economic analysis to expose how misuse of power, and not necessarily poverty, corrupts: "[T]he greatest wrongs in our government are perpetuated by rich men, the wire pulling agents of corporations and monopolies, in which the poor and the ignorant have no part." . . .

The last two decades of Anthony's life were as filled with rigorous lecture schedules and state-by-state campaigns as were the first two of her public career. In 1891, suffragist women throughout the United States came together to restore the Anthony home for her and to present her with a lifetime annuity. From then on, her unrelenting traveling and lectures were matters of will, not economic necessity. In her utopian vision she continued to be future-oriented for the movement. She tried to prepare women leaders to take over after she was gone, and she raised a fund to continue the work for woman suffrage after her death. In her work she created a legacy for women. When in 1900 at the age of eighty, she turned over the presidency of the National American Woman Suffrage Association to Carrie Lane Chapman Catt, Lane Catt acknowledged, "Miss Anthony will never have a successor." As her speeches grew shorter in the last few years of her life, Anthony's presence now conveyed her message. One month before her death at 86, she mustered enough strength to attend the annual suffrage convention. She left the movement and her cause with the optimism of her last words in public, "Failure is impossible!"

CHAPTER 3

ANTHONY'S RELATIONSHIPS WITH HER COLLEAGUES

PEOPLE
WHO MADE
HISTORY

SUSAN B. ANTHONY

Personal Animosity Within the Suffrage Movement

Judith E. Harper

In the following selection from her book *Susan B. Anthony: A Biographical Companion*, Judith E. Harper traces the demise of Anthony's friendship with suffragist Lucy Stone, including the far-reaching effect that their mutual antagonism had on the women's rights movement. According to Harper, the first seeds of discontent were sown when Anthony chastised Stone over her decision to briefly retire from suffrage work in order to marry and start a family. Both women felt personally injured by the other, Harper explains, and their festering resentment added fuel to the growing disparity in their political and ideological views. The 1869 split between the moderate and radical factions of the women's rights movement was due in part to the personal animosity that had developed between Stone and Anthony, she concludes.

As one of the earliest pioneers of the women's rights movement, acknowledged leader of the American Woman Suffrage Association (AWSA), publisher of the most illustrious and longest-lived women's rights journal (the *Woman's Journal*), and inexhaustible campaigner for woman suffrage for more than 40 years, Lucy Stone is recognized along with Susan B. Anthony and Elizabeth Cady Stanton as one of the three most preeminent of nineteenth-century American suffragists. The ups and downs of Stone's long and exceedingly complex relationship with Anthony, ranging from their close, sisterly friendship of the 1850s to the bitter and resentful feuding from the late 1860s on, help illuminate the deep, bitter conflicts driving the split in the woman suffrage movement, a division that lasted from 1869 until 1890.

STONE'S BACKGROUND

The daughter of a Massachusetts farmer, Stone struggled to receive an education against the wishes of her father. After completing her public schooling, Stone earned all the money for her higher education by teaching. Determined to attend college, Stone waited nine years before she had acquired the money to enroll at Oberlin College in Ohio. Inspired by abolitionists Sarah and Angelina Grimké and Abby Kelley Foster, Stone decided to become an antislavery and women's rights activist after her 1847 graduation from Oberlin. She was the first Massachusetts woman to obtain a college degree.

Stone commenced her career in reform in 1848 as a lecturing agent for the American Anti-Slavery Society (AASS). She was soon conquering the societal restriction barring women from speaking in public by delivering antislavery lectures throughout the Northeast. Her natural, unstudied, commonsense eloquence charmed audiences. Contemporary critics marveled over the extraordinary quality of her voice. In a field in which most great lecturers were men spouting fiery oratory, Stone's remarkably soothing, musical voice was a valuable asset, especially when speaking before hostile, proslavery audiences. She soon became one of the AASS's most popular lecturers, occasionally sharing equal billing with two of the abolitionist movement's most powerful orators, Wendell Phillips and William Lloyd Garrison.

Stone could not resist mingling women's rights issues and themes with her antislavery message. To her and to fellow feminist abolitionists Lucretia Coffin Mott and Kelley Foster, it was nearly impossible to differentiate the issues of political and social domination that enslaved African Americans from those that subjugated and oppressed women. At the insistence of the AASS leadership, Stone agreed to address women's rights concerns and abolitionist issues in separate lectures. Thus began Stone's extremely successful, lucrative career as a women's rights lecturer. She also devoted herself to organizing and executing a leadership role in the early national woman's rights conventions.

Anthony attributed her conversion to the cause of women's rights to Stone's speech at the First National Woman's Rights Convention held in Worcester, Massachusetts, in 1850, which Anthony later read in the *New York Tribune*. After reading it, she longed to meet Stone and other key luminaries of the women's rights movement. In 1851, at the home of

Cady Stanton, Anthony was first introduced to Stone at a meeting to brainstorm ideas for a People's College, a coeducational venture. From that point on, Stone and Anthony frequently corresponded. Their early letters reflect their opinions, determination, fears, and problems concerning their wearing of the controversial Bloomer costume. As the more seasoned activist, Stone's letters to Anthony were filled with friendly advice and encouragement, often countermanding Anthony's image of herself as an inadequate lecturer and reformer. Their later letters illustrate their mutual passion for women's rights reform as well as their increasing personal closeness, their exchange of deeply personal feelings, and their warm affection. Anthony greatly admired Stone's breadth of knowledge about abolitionism, her oratorical prowess, her thriving career, and her impassioned devotion to women's rights. For all these reasons, Anthony was extremely optimistic about their future together as women's rights crusaders.

Anthony was shocked and devastated when she learned that both Stone and another close friend and fellow activist, Antoinette Brown, intended to marry. In 1855, Stone became engaged to Cincinnati abolitionist and businessman Henry Blackwell, and not long afterward, Brown promised to marry Samuel Blackwell, Henry's brother. Anthony could not believe that Stone, who had so vehemently sworn herself to a life of single independence, could so easily give up her reform career. Despite Stone's and Brown's protestations to the contrary, Anthony perceived marriage as the death knell of a woman's activism. She knew from her married sisters' and Cady Stanton's experiences that the demands of marriage, the management of a household, and the bearing and raising of children severely limited a woman's freedom to travel and would obliterate their ability to participate in arduous women's rights campaigns. Anthony interpreted Stone's decision to marry as betrayal and abandonment—leaving Anthony to fight the women's rights battle alone. Stone was hurt and bewildered by Anthony's resentment and at first tried to prove that she was as committed to women's rights as ever. Although marriage would not reduce Stone's ardor or her allegiance to women's rights, the 1857 birth of her daughter, Alice Stone Blackwell, did prevent her from active involvement in the movement until 1866.

Anthony, perhaps overwhelmed by the demands of leading the campaign for the New York Married Women's Property Law and her commitments as New York agent of the AASS, wrote stern letters to Stone, nagging and disapproving of her decision to retire temporarily to raise her daughter. Anthony's words wounded Stone, who was already struggling with her new roles as wife and mother and with her isolation from her reform colleagues. Although she was in desperate need of understanding from old friends, she would not find support for her domestic life from Anthony. Both women's unresolved anger and pain seriously eroded their bond. Yet despite the slowly festering resentment on both sides, Stone and Anthony continued to correspond—Stone to encourage and applaud Anthony's achievements,

THE EFFECTS OF DOMESTIC LIFE

A professor emeritus of historical studies from the University of California at Santa Cruz, Page Smith describes Susan B. Anthony's assumption that her colleagues could not balance their work in the women's rights movement and their family obligations. Smith's numerous books include the eight-volume People's History of the United States *and* Daughters of the Promised Land: Women in American History, *from which the following passage is excerpted.*

Nette Brown Blackwell produced a baby girl scarcely a year after her marriage and Lucy Stone had a daughter a few months later. The births seemed to confirm Susan Anthony's anxieties about the effects of domestic life on these two stalwarts of the cause. When Nette had her second child, another girl, Susan left her off the program of the woman's rights convention on the grounds that her domestic responsibilities would probably keep her away. Nette wrote indignantly to Susan that "the public has nothing to do with my babies or my home affairs. It may take care of its own personal interests as best it may. I will do the same." . . .

Even Elizabeth Cady Stanton let Susan down. After being cited to Nette as an example of a reformer who had had her children early in order to leave her career unhampered by the care of infants, Elizabeth Cady, in her early forties became pregnant once again. "For a *moment's pleasure* to herself or her husband," Susan B. Anthony wrote despairingly to Nette, Elizabeth had greatly increased "the *load* of *cares* under which she already groans."

Page Smith, *Daughters of the Promised Land: Women in American History*, 1970.

Anthony to inform Stone of developments in her and others' women's rights campaigns. In 1863, Stone consented to Anthony's request that she preside at the convention that formed the Woman's National Loyal League (WNLL). Although Anthony hoped that leading the meeting would push Stone back into the vanguard of reform, Stone remained firm about her exclusive commitment to her family.

Following the Civil War, as Stone's school-age daughter needed her less, she rejoiced at having more time for women's rights work. She was actively involved in helping Anthony and Cady Stanton organize and execute the Eleventh National Woman's Rights Convention in 1866, at which the American Equal Rights Association (AERA) was formed. Stone and Henry Blackwell were leaders of the AERA, along with Anthony, Cady Stanton, Parker Pillsbury, Frederick Douglass, and other former abolitionists. In 1866 and 1867, Stone and Henry Blackwell worked closely with Anthony and Cady Stanton to counter efforts by Phillips, Douglass, and other predominantly male Republican AERA members who determined that obtaining civil and political rights for African-American males must take priority over woman suffrage. In the spring of 1867, Stone responded to Anthony's pleas that she lead an AERA woman suffrage campaign in Kansas. In November, Kansans were to vote on two suffrage referenda—to enfranchise African-American males and all women.

BITTER DIVISIONS

In the fall of 1867, months after she and Blackwell returned from Kansas, Stone was enraged to discover that Anthony had teamed up with the anti–African-American Democrat George Francis Train in the final months of the Kansas campaign. Stone could not fathom how Anthony could have reneged on her principles and her years of dedication to African-American rights to join forces with a racist. But what was even more heinous in Stone's view was the fact that Anthony used equal rights money to pay for the Train campaign without consulting her or any other AERA members. When Anthony returned east, Stone, Blackwell, and other members of the AERA executive committee harshly confronted her at a private AERA meeting, berating her for her alliance with Train and the resultant misuse of AERA funds. According to Stone, Anthony retorted, "I AM the Equal

Rights Association. Not one of you amounts to shucks except for me." This response, perhaps the result of being called on the carpet by members who had not devoted every waking minute to woman suffrage and African-American rights as she had for the last 13 years, only confirmed Stone and Blackwell's opinion of Anthony's despotic tendencies and unwillingness to share leadership.

By 1868, Stone and Blackwell had joined forces with Phillips and New England Republican AERA members who postponed agitating for woman suffrage to push through the Fifteenth Amendment. Stone and Blackwell then established the pro-Republican, Boston-based New England Woman Suffrage Association (NEWSA). Its first goal was to secure the franchise for African-American men through the Fifteenth Amendment. Meanwhile, Anthony and Cady Stanton's anti-Republican, pro-Democratic rhetoric and radical feminism as broadcast in their newspaper *The Revolution,* along with Stone and Blackwell's anti-Anthony and anti-*Revolution* protests, intensified the divisiveness among AERA members and women's rights reformers, causing the once-united group to split into two factions.

Stone and Blackwell were enraged by Anthony and Cady Stanton's formation of the National Woman Suffrage Association (NWSA) in May 1869 and by what they perceived as their purposeful exclusion from it. Stone immediately initiated plans for a separate national suffrage organization for conservative and moderate female and male suffragists who supported the Fifteenth Amendment and were either offended by *The Revolution* or estranged from Anthony and Cady Stanton because of it. Although *The Revolution*'s radicalism distressed her, Stone was more opposed to what she perceived as its anti–African-American agenda and its endorsement of the Democratic Party. To rally a membership for their new organization, soon to be named the American Woman Suffrage Association (AWSA), Stone and Blackwell appealed to all women's rights activists, including many who were longtime friends and allies of Anthony and Cady Stanton.

Like Anthony, Stone recognized the ability of the press to influence and educate the public. She also began preparations to launch a women's rights newspaper that would rival *The Revolution* and provide an alternative publication for more moderate and conservative women's rights activists. The *Woman's Journal* was first published in Boston on January 8, 1870, two years to the day after the first publication of *The Revolution.*

None of the reconciliation attempts of the early 1870s tempted Stone, undoubtedly because none tackled the thorniest issues that had compelled her to form a separate organization. In addition to their considerable ideological differences, Stone was convinced that she could not trust Anthony or Cady Stanton. She was also opposed to most of their radical stands on women's rights issues such as marriage and divorce reform, the unionization of labor, labor reform, and prostitution. Stone had always been highly critical of Cady Stanton's work on divorce reform. Since Cady Stanton had first proposed massive changes in marriage and divorce law in 1860, Stone had agreed with Phillips that divorce reform was not women's rights. As the years passed and throughout Stone's decades of leadership in the AWSA, she struggled to keep the AWSA focused only on woman suffrage. She pushed aside what she considered to be marginal, radical women's rights issues that alienated moderate and conservative Americans from woman suffrage. Consequently, Stone wasted no time worrying about unification with the NWSA, instead focusing her energies on developing a vital national organization.

In 1872, Anthony, Cady Stanton, and the NWSA backed the Republican Party presidential candidate, Ulysses S. Grant. Since ever-loyal Republicans Stone and Henry Blackwell were also supporting him, Anthony wrote to Stone inviting her to consider a joint campaign. When Stone refused, Anthony was dejected. It was her last personal attempt to move closer to Stone.

Although the NWSA's and the AWSA's separate goals and areas of emphasis kept them from colliding in the field for the most part, the leaders of both organizations were acutely aware of the competitive rivalry between them. Both NWSA and AWSA leaders accused their rivals of deliberately undermining them, but in reality each organization tried to "steal" or drum up membership in the other's backyard, and each was guilty of exaggerating its achievements while neglecting to mention its competitors' contributions. Oddly enough, Anthony and Cady Stanton as well as Stone and Blackwell interpreted these political maneuvers as personal affronts and insults—a pattern that underscores the intensity of their interpersonal relationships and the traumatic nature of the original split.

MOVING TOWARD A MERGER

By 1886, Stone found herself approving of and praising the achievements of NWSA leaders, who she believed were finally beginning to help the cause of woman suffrage. Factions in both the AWSA and NWSA were eager to explore the possibilities of cooperating on campaigns and projects and coordinating a merger. In December 1887, with the prodding and impetus provided by the younger generation of suffragists in both organizations, Stone and Anthony attended a meeting to discuss unification. More than two years of negotiation later, the woman suffrage movement was united under the banner of the new National American Woman Suffrage Association (NAWSA).

Stone was gravely disappointed by Cady Stanton's assumption of the presidency of the NAWSA. Throughout the negotiations, Stone had been adamant about one issue—that she, Anthony, and Cady Stanton abstain from the leadership of the new organization. But when the new NAWSA membership kept clamoring for either Cady Stanton or Anthony to be president, Anthony took advantage of the opportunity to maneuver Cady Stanton into the presidency, thus maintaining her (Anthony's) primary role and the NWSA's top leadership structure.

Stone chose not to confront Anthony directly concerning the NAWSA leadership issue. She maintained an externally positive, laudatory public attitude toward the NAWSA, but inwardly she was seething. Stone's and Anthony's pattern of avoiding rather than mediating areas of interpersonal turmoil, first established in the late 1850s, not only characterized their 35-year relationship but also contributed to the divergent natures, functions, and agendas of the AWSA and the NWSA.

NO PERSONAL RECONCILIATION

As far as Stone and Anthony's relationship was concerned, not much had changed by the time of the merger. From the late 1860s until Stone's death in 1893, each woman regularly confided to friends that she was repeatedly hurt by the other's words and actions. Biographies of Stone and Anthony abound with anecdotes of both women being stunned by the nasty comments their friends had supposedly overheard each woman say about the other. Neither Stone nor Anthony appears to have confronted the other directly about the veracity of such rumors, nor did either woman approach the other about the possibility of resolving their differences. They both chose instead to rage in private and vent their angst to their friends.

Despite the intensity of their conflicts, Stone and Anthony shared one striking characteristic—their single-minded, wholehearted passion and undivided devotion to the cause of women's rights and woman suffrage. In a letter to Alice Blackwell in 1887, Stone explained to her daughter: "Its [the cause's] success and prosperity have always been more to me, than any personal feeling, and any damage to IT far more than any personal ill will, or misunderstanding of myself, so I could always rejoice in good work no matter who did it."

Anthony's Attitude Toward Men

Lynn Sherr

A national correspondent for *ABC News* and *20/20*,
Lynn Sherr is the coauthor of *Susan B. Anthony Slept
Here: A Guide to American Women's Landmarks*. In
the following excerpt from her book *Failure Is Impossible: Susan B. Anthony in Her Own Words*, Sherr
examines the popular misconception that Anthony
universally hated men. While Anthony did not hesi-
tate to criticize men's sexist behavior, the author
maintains, she did not hold all men responsible for
the inequality of women. In fact, Sherr reveals,
Anthony cultivated close friendships and working
relationships with many male politicians and social
reformers who supported the cause of women's rights.

Susan B. Anthony has a way of saying the word "male," observed a reporter at a Congressional committee in 1870, "so
that it sounds like the snapping of small arms." Indeed, the
follies and practices of the men running the government and
writing rude reviews about her work provided stores of am-
munition for her suffrage wars. And she does seem to have
enjoyed entertaining friends and colleagues at the expense
of some poor man's ineptitude. In *The Revolution*, the newspaper she published, the following item appeared in 1869:

> Miss Susan B. Anthony considers it her mission to keep the
> world, or at least her part of it, in hot water. Gentlemen,
> take notice.

And an Indiana newspaper reporter made these observa-
tions after hearing her lecture on The Cause.

> It has become quite the fashion for suffrage lecturers to flat-
> ter men until they, the men, leave the audience room with a
> better opinion of themselves than they had when they en-
> tered it. Miss Anthony is not guilty of any such lobbying.

Notwithstanding her unquestioned justice, we doubt if the vanity of the men who hear her is very much inflated. They slink out after the lecture, looking very much as though they had been well whipped.

But she did not hate all men and, more important, did not blame them all for the inequities of the ruling majority. The only thing a man had to do to win Susan B. Anthony's respect—and eternal loyalty—was to be fair. That is, to understand that women were people, too, who deserved equal rights. There were plenty who qualified.

The list begins with her father and includes many of the abolitionists who remained close friends despite their behavior over the Fourteenth Amendment. One of the first men to sign up for The Cause was Henry Blackwell, who cemented his commitment by marrying Lucy Stone. Their daughter, Alice Stone Blackwell, would help lead the second generation to the vote. Anthony introduced Henry at a suffrage convention in 1900 with these teasing, but very grateful, words:

Here is a man who has the virtue of having stood by the woman's cause for nearly fifty years. I can remember him when his hair was not white, and when he was following up our conventions assiduously because a bright, little, red-cheeked woman attracted him. She attracted him so strongly that he still works for woman suffrage, and will do so as long as he lives, not only because of her who was always so true and faithful to the cause—Lucy Stone—but also because he has a daughter, a worthy representative of the twain who were made one.

POLITICAL ALLIES

The honor roll goes on, with special standing reserved for the members of Congress who went out of their way to introduce or support legislation in favor of a suffrage amendment. Representative George W. Julian of Indiana and Senator Samuel C. Pomeroy of Kansas made the first resolutions for proposal in 1868. Senators Henry W. Blair of New Hampshire, Aaron Sargent of California (later ambassador to Germany), and Thomas W. Palmer of Michigan, to name a favored few, remained staunch advocates. At a hearing in 1892, she singled out Senator George F. Hoar of Massachusetts for presenting the first favorable suffrage report to the Senate fifteen years earlier. According to one account, "Laurel wreaths and bouquets would have been Senator Hoar's portion if they had been available."

MEN'S DEBT TO SUSAN B. ANTHONY

In the following excerpt from her book Susan B. Anthony: The Woman Who Changed the Mind of a Nation, *author and suffragist Rheta Childe Dorr asserts that men as well as women owe a lasting debt to Anthony for helping to free women from their dependence on men.*

It is to men as well as women that I have wanted to present Susan B. Anthony as a warm and living, faulty, but human and dynamic personality, for men also owe her a great and lasting debt. In the weak and helpless, dependent women of her youth Susan saw something worse than mere chattels of men; she saw a burden that had to be lifted from the shoulders of men. She loved liberty for itself, and she gave her life as much to free the slave owner as the slave. For this Susan B. Anthony deserves to be remembered, not merely as a great name, but as a woman possessing that feminine and emotional sense of humanity which transcends class and sex and embraces with love the whole human race.

Rheta Childe Dorr, *Susan B. Anthony: The Woman Who Changed the Mind of a Nation*, 1928.

As a seasoned political operative, Susan B. Anthony perfectly understood how to use her allies. She was quite pleased with her team's ability to turn support into action:

> [W]e once induced one of our good friends, ex-Senator Palmer, of Michigan, to deliver a speech on woman suffrage on the floor of the Senate. It was an excellent speech, but no better than I have heard Mrs. [Elizabeth Cady] Stanton and others of our leading women make. If any of them had made it, nobody would have heard of it again, because everyone would have said, "Oh, it's only a woman's talk." When Senator Palmer spoke, however, the whole country had to listen. The press associations sent off a third of a column or so of condensed abstract; the *Congressional Record* contained the full text of the speech; the daily newspapers of Michigan made copious extracts from it and comments on it; and every weekly paper in that State, except one, published it entire. The same tactics have been used with other public men of note who are friendly to our cause. Speaker [Thomas B.] Reed [of Maine] is one who has made some splendid efforts in our behalf, and what he has said has gone everywhere.

Anthony applauded a wide array of male benefactors and eagerly attended the founding meeting of the Spinner

Memorial Association, a group of women honoring General Francis E. Spinner, the first person to hire women for posts in the federal government. She was not aware that his gesture, as U.S. Treasury secretary, was motivated by the realization that female employees would work for less money. But then, everyone has to start somewhere.

The New Generation: Anthony's Search for a Successor

Eleanor Flexner

As Susan B. Anthony grew older, she began to look for a successor to whom she could safely pass the reins of the women's suffrage movement. Ultimately, she found not one but two capable women: Carrie Chapman Catt and Anna Howard Shaw. Both of these women had markedly different talents and leadership styles, author Eleanor Flexner explains, yet each was instrumental in upholding Anthony's legacy until the battle for women's right to vote was finally won. The following piece is taken from Flexner's *Century of Struggle: The Woman's Rights Movement in the United States*, originally published in 1959 and considered to be the first professional history of the women's suffrage movement.

The aging Susan Anthony was not one to hold power to herself; she watched for lieutenants with ability to whom she could hand over her post, especially after the merger of the two suffrage associations in 1890. The suffrage cause was fortunate that she found two, who between them divided the leadership of the movement until the goal had been won.

ANTHONY'S TWO SUCCESSORS

Both came from the growing numbers of college-trained women. Both were from the Middle West; one was of first-generation pioneer stock, the other only a little less removed from the physical actualities of the frontier. At this point resemblance between the lives of Carrie Chapman Catt and Anna Howard Shaw ceases, save for the fact that woman suffrage became the main focus of their lives.

Carrie Lane was born on a Wisconsin farm in 1859; her

Reprinted by permission of the publisher from *Century of Struggle: The Woman's Rights Movement in the United States*, by Eleanor Flexner and Ellen Fitzpatrick, pages 229–32 (Cambridge, MA: Harvard University Press). Copyright © 1959, 1975 by Eleanor Flexner; © 1996 by the President and Fellows of Harvard College.

family moved to northeastern Iowa when some of the land was still unploughed prairie. She graduated from Iowa State College and served in rapid succession as teacher, school administrator, and journalist, first on a small Iowa town paper and then in San Francisco. When her first husband, Leo Chapman, died of typhoid fever only a few months after their marriage, she turned to lecturing and suffrage work in her home state of Iowa, where her work soon attracted the notice of state leaders. The year 1890 which produced a united suffrage movement marked her entrance into national work, and her marriage to George Catt, a successful engineer and staunch adherent of suffrage who made it possible for his wife to give more and more of her time to it.

It soon became apparent to Miss Anthony that here was not only an able speaker, but a woman with tremendous potentialities as an organizer, something the suffrage movement notably lacked in Miss Anthony's later years. After trying her wings in some grueling campaigns, notably the South Dakota fiasco of 1890 and the victorious Colorado campaign of 1893, and making a report at the 1895 annual convention which flayed the suffrage association for its omissions and shortcomings, Mrs. Catt was made chairman of a newly instituted Organization Committee. Here, for the next five years, she had abundant and heartbreaking opportunity to develop the flair for planning, for check-up and detail, and for seeking out and training fresh leadership, which were to be the hallmarks of her suffrage work for a quarter of a century.

The young organizer displayed considerable brashness in some of the methods she attempted to introduce in an organization which had always operated in a highly personal and haphazard manner: definite plans of work for local groups; state headquarters; study courses in, of all things, political science and economics; a manual of organization; a consistent membership system (something no one had ever bothered about); and soundly based national association finances (a goal not to be achieved for twenty years). Yet Mrs. Catt, far in advance of anyone else, saw these things as essential to any kind of sustained, consistent work, and to final success. She labored for nine years to lay some kind of sound organizational basis for a sprawling movement of women with conflicting demands on their time and energies, and with many inhibitions, even when they believed strongly in their cause. It was unrewarding, killing work, ahead of its time. But suffragists got a whiff of organization and discipline which some of them remembered later in their hour of need. . . .

When the time came for Miss Anthony to step down in 1900, Mrs. Catt was the older leader's choice to succeed her as president of the National American Woman Suffrage Association, by sheer weight of merit over any personal preference; the decision was a painful one since the woman who was Mrs. Catt's only possible opponent was Susan Anthony's closest friend and co-worker for the last twenty years of her life.

Anna Howard Shaw had known a pioneer childhood of great hardship, and difficult years as a divinity student. At the age of thirty-five, feeling that her hardwon Cape Cod parish was becoming too comfortable a rut, she entered a Boston medical school and received an M.D. degree in 1886. Her experience with the impoverished women of the Boston slums, in the dual role of preacher and physician, convinced her that their basic problem was one neither religion nor medicine alone could solve:

> In my association with the women of the streets, I realized the limitations of my work in the ministry and in medicine. As minister to soul and body one could do little for these women. For such as them, one's efforts must begin at the very foundation of the social structure. Laws for them must be made and enforced, and some of those laws could only be made and enforced by women.

She began to lecture for the Women's Christian Temperance Union (W.C.T.U.), becoming a close friend of Frances Willard's, and also for the Massachusetts Woman Suffrage Association. For several years after leaving ministerial work she headed the W.C.T.U.'s suffrage department. Miss Anthony marked her originally for her gifts as a speaker; the great age of woman orators had come and gone, and for a quarter of a century Dr. Shaw was unmatched in eloquence and effectiveness. She soon gave up other causes, and made the winning of suffrage her life work, although for years she was obliged to go on lecturing for her livelihood.

But when Miss Anthony retired, suffrage needed an orator less than it did an organizer and a leader who was free to give the cause her undivided efforts. To say that Anna Howard Shaw was disappointed is an understatement. But she recognized the inevitability of the decision and continued to give her not inconsiderable best. Without close domestic ties and responsibilities, she became as peripatetic as ever Susan Anthony had been, and for years traveled up and down the land, the most sought-after speaker in every state campaign and every gathering whose aim was the women's vote.

"AUNT SUSAN"

Anthony created her own family of women friends and coworkers, Lynn Sherr writes in the following excerpt from her book Failure Is Impossible: Susan B. Anthony in Her Own Words. *In particular, she maintains, Anthony enjoyed the admiration of the younger generation of suffragists, whom she considered her adoptive nieces.*

The women in Susan B. Anthony's life *were* her family. She revered the leadership of Lucretia Mott and the legacy of Mary Wollstonecraft. She wore a ring from pioneering physician Dr. Clemence Lozier and a dress from Mormon women in Utah. . . . She traveled, worked, commiserated, plotted, planned, and revolutionized with her female friends, transforming the world with such reformers-in-arms as Lucy Stone, Paulina Wright Davis, Amelia Bloomer, and Antoinette Brown Blackwell. . . .

There was a special place in Anthony's heart for her younger colleagues—a rotating cadre of admiring workers whom she trained, then depended upon, to carry on the job. Known as "Susan's Girls," they were allowed to call her "Aunt Susan" and included such future leaders as Carrie Chapman Catt and the Reverend Ann Howard Shaw, both of whom would succeed Anthony as president of the suffrage association.

Lynn Sherr, *Failure Is Impossible: Susan B. Anthony in Her Own Words*, 1995.

After four years, Mrs. Catt resigned the presidency of the suffrage association: she was worn out from ten years' grueling effort, and ill health in her family had become a grave concern (Mr. Catt died the following year). There was also another reason for her withdrawal: her role in the growing international suffrage movement.

The latter owed its original impetus to Susan Anthony, who had visited Great Britain in 1884 with Mrs. Elizabeth Cady Stanton, and broached the idea of an international suffrage association to British leaders. The organization of the International Council of Women and its several Congresses in 1888, 1893 and 1902 served to forward the idea; beginning in 1902, Mrs. Catt undertook to bring about its realization.

The International Woman Suffrage Alliance was launched at
a congress held in Berlin in June 1904 with eight affiliates:
Australia, Denmark, Germany, Great Britain, the Nether-
lands, Norway, Sweden, and the United States. The last continued to furnish leadership for the Alliance, in the person of
Mrs. Catt, until 1923.

In 1904 Dr. Shaw stepped into the presidency of the National American Woman Suffrage Association, a post she
was to hold for eleven years. Susan B. Anthony was still alive
and active: she had attended the Berlin Congress which
founded the International Alliance, and while she was no
longer the functioning head of the movement in the United
States, she remained its vital center.

ANTHONY'S FINAL ACCOMPLISHMENT

She was in harness until her last illness during the annual
suffrage convention in 1906 held in Baltimore; even then, ill
as she was, she held out long enough to win a promise from
M. Carey Thomas, the president of Bryn Mawr College, and
her close friend, Miss Mary Garrett, that they would raise a
fund of $60,000 which would support Dr. Shaw for a five-
year period, so that suffrage work would not suffer from her
lecturing for a livelihood. One month after this last service to
the cause which had been her life, Miss Anthony was dead.
Her passing marked the end of an era. She was the last of the
giants who had launched the struggle to improve the condition of women to leave the scene. She had lived and worked,
without respite and without discouragement, through the
years of ridicule, vilification, and apparent hopelessness,
which today are all but forgotten. When she died, few thinking people denied either the logic or the inevitability of
woman suffrage. The only question that remained was,
"When?"

The Patron Saint of the Suffrage Movement

Sara Hunter Graham

During Susan B. Anthony's final years, the younger members of the women's rights movement tended to idolize her as a beloved leader and pioneer suffragist, according to former Louisiana State University history professor Sara Hunter Graham. At the same time, Graham writes, the younger suffragists downplayed Anthony's radicalism and stressed her qualities that corresponded with traditional feminine ideals. This trend increased sharply after Anthony's death in 1906. Her bereaved colleagues and followers sincerely mourned Anthony with an outpouring of tributes to her memory, but in Graham's opinion, they also further sanitized her image as a saintly and self-sacrificing reformer. The following reading is excerpted from Graham's book *Woman Suffrage and the New Democracy*.

As past president of the National American Woman Suffrage Association (NAWSA) and a representative of pioneer activism, Susan B. Anthony had attained celebrity status within the suffrage movement long before her death. The annual NAWSA conventions were carefully scheduled to coincide with her birthday, and convention-goers could count on lavish celebrations, emotional speeches, and a personal word or two from the celebrity herself. In addition to her appearances at the annual conventions, Anthony had traveled extensively for years and was well known to suffragists throughout America, who increasingly viewed her as the living embodiment of their cause. Local fund-raisers often took the form of "Susan B. Anthony Day," and state suffrage convention badges and programs routinely bore her picture. Such was her stature in the movement that during her later

From *Woman Suffrage and the New Democracy*, by Sara Hunter Graham. Copyright © 1996 by Yale University. Reprinted by permission of the publisher, Yale University Press.

years she often witnessed her own apotheosis. In 1903, for example, while dining on bluefish and "diplomate pudding" with a Brooklyn, New York, suffrage league, she heard a series of speeches presented on the topic "Susan B. Anthony: Lessons and Inspirations from Her Life."

Ida Husted Harper was in part responsible for Anthony's transformation from reviled fanatic to adored leader. Her two-volume biography of the reformer was published in 1898, and it provided readers with the day-to-day occurrences of her subject's life in almost Boswellian detail. A third volume, added after Anthony's death, extended the work to more than 1,600 pages and included excerpts from over a hundred highly favorable editorials on Anthony that appeared after her death. In addition to her work as a hagiographer, Harper proved to be unsurpassed as a nascent press agent. In keeping with NAWSA's new emphasis on respectability, she composed an article in 1903 for *Pearson's Magazine* entitled "Miss Anthony at Home" that portrayed the aging suffragist as "domestic in every fiber of her body." With an eye to her prospective audience, Harper cloaked her subject in the rhetoric of domesticity with such feminine attributes as neatness, hospitality, self-sacrifice, patience, and loyalty. According to the article, Anthony sat down at the breakfast table looking "like a lovely grandmother," to a meal "strictly of the feminine order." Later she embarked upon a day of womanly pursuits that included cooking, cleaning, and sewing. "Miss Anthony," concluded the article, "never has suggested ways for repairing the damages of society with one-half the skill she employed in teaching her nieces her wonderful method of darning rents in garments and household linens." Through her literary efforts, Harper helped to replace the stereotypical image of masculinized fanatic with a nonthreatening feminine heroine imbued with domestic virtues.

The sanctification of Susan B. Anthony was not completed until her death in 1906. At that year's convention, the aging reformer appeared before her devoted disciples for the last time. Her health gone, she exhorted the delegates in a faltering voice to continue in the great work begun at Seneca Falls, New York, and closed her remarks with the words, "Failure is impossible!" After the convention, she traveled to Washington to attend the annual congressional hearings on the proposed suffrage amendment but was too ill to leave her bed. Returning to her home in Rochester, New York, Anthony was attended by her niece and sister and, in her final hours, by Anna Howard Shaw. Profoundly shaken by the loss of her closest friend, Shaw would help to create the most enduring and vital of suffrage traditions: the suffrage saint.

THE CREATION OF THE DEATHBED SCENE

Like Harper, Anna Howard Shaw was uniquely fitted to the role of hagiographer. She met Anthony at a suffrage meeting in 1888, and a lifelong friendship had ensued. Shaw clearly worshipped the older woman. One of her favorite stories featured the seventy-year old Anthony, wrapped in a dressing gown and talking until dawn, "foreseeing everything, forgetting nothing, and sweeping me with her in her flight toward our common goal until I . . . experienced an almost dizzy sense of exhilaration." Such was Shaw's devotion that in her 1915 autobiography, Anthony figures almost as prominently as does the author herself. As both president of NAWSA and an Anthony disciple, Shaw hurried to Rochester when word came that the end was near. What followed would provide an important source of inspiration for the cult of personality that adopted Anthony as its patron saint.

Susan B. Anthony

Deathbed scenes were a popular literary device for turn-of-the-century novelists, and it is therefore not surprising that Shaw chose to record the scene she witnessed in both the periodical press and in her autobiography. Indeed, her vivid description of Anthony's pale visage and prophetic words lend credence to the expression "life imitates art." Two passages in particular express the motif Shaw sought to capture. On the last afternoon of her life, Anthony suddenly began to recite the names of the women who had worked for women's rights over the years. The women of this "final roll-call . . . seemed to file past her dying eyes that day in an endless, shadowy review," Shaw wrote. She quoted Anthony as saying "I know the sacrifices they have made, but it has all been worth while!" With this benediction, Anthony lapsed into silence for a time, but she rallied once more to assure Shaw that, after death, she would continue to be an active force in the woman suffrage movement. "Who knows?" she speculated, "Perhaps I may be able to do more for the Cause after I am gone than while I am here."

In a sense she was right. Anthony's vision (or Shaw's invention?) of "the shadowy review," coupled with her prophecy of a kind of mystic activism beyond the grave, suggests a type of secular sanctification well known to readers of sentimental fiction of the period. The theme of suffrage saint was also conspicuous in a selection of poems written about Anthony and published after her death in volume 3 of Harper's biography. "She is not dead but more alive / than in her fairest earthly days," one poet proclaimed, while another pictured her "with eyes that looked beyond the gates of death" and crowned by a "halo of her venerable age." Perhaps the most explicit example of sanctification was by John Russell Hayes, who poetically recorded Anthony's entry into a supernatural suffrage procession:

> And then my vision faded,
> And a lordly melody rolled
> As down celestial vistas
> The saintly company strolled.
> But the face of that latest comer
> I longest kept in sight—
> So ardent with consecration,
> So lit with angelic light: . . .

> Crowned is she and sainted
> In heavenly halls above
> Who freely gave for her sisters
> A life of boundless love.

On March 15, 1906, the suffrage saint was buried in Rochester, New York. The mayor of Rochester, the president of Rochester University, and other local dignitaries were present, in addition to suffrage and temperance leaders, aging abolitionists, college women, friends, and family members. Despite a heavy snowfall, an estimated crowd of ten thousand assembled outside the church, pressing against the doors and windows to hear Anna Howard Shaw's eulogy. Touching briefly on Anthony's "womanly attributes," she then described her subject's heroism and devotion to the cause. "There is no death for such as she," Shaw concluded, and she predicted that "the ages will come to revere her name." When the church doors were opened at the close of the service, crowds of mourners streamed past the body. One mourner in particular caught the attention of some reporters: an elderly black woman, covered with snow and leaning heavily on a crutch, paused by the coffin and sobbed aloud into a frost-covered handkerchief. Other journalists chose to feature an aged black man, also limping, who took as a memento mori a single leaf from the funeral wreath. The heroic eulogies, patriotic rhetoric, and weeping black spectators reminded some witnesses of another fallen emancipator. Describing the long line of mourners who filed past the body, one observer called them "the plain people, the people Susan B. Anthony and Abraham Lincoln loved." After the long procession had passed, a female honor guard from the university escorted the coffin past houses draped in black to the grave site where Shaw delivered the final words.

Memorial Services

In the days that followed, friends worked to ensure a lasting memory for their patron saint. Rochester educators named an elementary school after her, a local church commissioned a stained glass window bearing her likeness, and women's clubs, temperance groups, and civic organizations honored her with memorials. Ida Husted Harper collected more than a thousand editorials that eulogized Anthony, including one from the antisuffrage *New York Times* lauding "the tender, womanly loveliness of the great reformer." Suffragists across the nation held memorial services like the one that was conducted by the Kentucky Equal Rights Association (KERA) a week after Anthony's death. Mary Clay, a longtime suffragist and descendant of the Great Compromiser [American statesman and orator Henry Clay], presided over the service that took place in the Clay family home. In the center of the parlor draped in yellow satin and black crepe stood a large picture of Susan B. Anthony, flanked by a small candle in a pink candlestick, a souvenir from the suffrage leader's eightieth birthday celebration. On a nearby table was a smaller portrait of the reformer, surrounded by photographs of other pioneers like Lucy Stone and Isabella Beecher Hooker. After a roll call of pioneer suffragists and a sketch of the reformer's work for women's rights, the assembly heard a series of elegies and a dramatic reading based on Anthony's final days. Following a rosary and benediction, the women sang "Nearer, My God, to Thee" and adjourned for refreshments.

The nature of the Kentucky memorial service closely follows the form routinely employed by literary, church, or civic gatherings of women, but with a suffrage theme. Within this structure, songs, poems, and dramatic readings provided a thread of continuity between old forms and new meanings. The intimate atmosphere of the parlor meeting encouraged participation by women who would have shied away from speaking to a large, mixed audience. Overtones of religious ritual endowed the service with both familiarity and stately respectability in accord with the tastes of the times. The parlor decor approached ecclesiastical parody with its makeshift altar and display of icons. In addition, the service followed a quasiliturgical pattern, employing both poetic and prose readings and ending with the litany of the rosary and the benediction.

Kentucky suffragists also shaped the memorial service to suit the private agenda of their movement. Tradition played an important role: the veneration of the pioneers, the idea of a parallel women's history, and the philosophy of female progress were all incorporated into the ceremony. In her posthumous role, Susan B. Anthony became what no living woman could be: a universally shared symbol of the cause whose very name could conjure a constellation of images and sentiment. Across the nation clubwomen and suffragists met for similar services. Within a decade Anthony had become, like Lincoln before her, part of the common mental property of Progressive Era Americans. Her picture was hung beside those of the Founding Fathers in schoolrooms across America, her memory achieving a measure of the vague immortality accorded to the heroes of American democracy. . . .

A New Image for a New Age

In the first decade of the twentieth century, suffrage leaders set out to create a new image for their movement. Their basic goal was to forge a notion of women's history and female progress that could be accepted as consonant with the wider aspirations of mainstream society. In a sense they banished the radical past, turned their back on nonconformity, and in the process captured the support of quietly influential groups of women. Gone was the taint of extremism that had haunted the movement for decades; the parlor meeting had adopted "Aunt Susan" as its patron saint, and suffragism had come of age.

DISCUSSION QUESTIONS

1. Geoffrey C. Ward describes the religious and moral atmosphere of Susan B. Anthony's childhood home, focusing especially on the influence of her Quaker father. In Ward's opinion, what aspects of the Quaker lifestyle and belief system are reflected in Anthony's career as a reformer?

2. According to Kathleen Barry's essay, Anthony's difficulties at boarding school impacted the development of her personality. What specific effects did this experience have on Anthony, in Barry's opinion? Which were positive and which negative? Explain, citing the text to support your answer.

3. Although Anthony began her career as a temperance worker, she soon abandoned that cause to devote her life to the women's rights movement. According to Miriam Gurko, what connections did Anthony see between the issues of temperance and women's rights? How did her experiences within the temperance movement solidify her decision to concentrate on the women's movement?

4. Katharine Anthony delineates two "epoch-making" changes brought about by Anthony's work in the abolitionist movement. What were these two changes? How did they affect Anthony's view of herself and the women's rights movement?

CHAPTER 2

1. According to Rheta Childe Dorr, what was the women's rights movement like before Anthony took over the reins? In what ways did Anthony alter the tactics and direction of the movement, and how did these changes benefit the cause?

2. At the start of the Civil War, the leaders of the women's rights movement chose to cease their activism for the duration of the war. According to Bill Severn, why did Anthony oppose this decision? How did it contribute to the

division in the women's movement after the Civil War? In what other ways did this decision prove counterproductive to the cause of women's rights?

3. In her article, Lynne Masel-Walters relates the history of the *Revolution*, the first major national publication concerning women's rights. What role did Anthony play in the formation and operation of the *Revolution*? How did the *Revolution* differ from other newspapers run by and for women? In Masel-Walters's opinion, what legacy did the *Revolution* leave?

4. Israel Kugler describes Anthony's activities in the labor movement during the late 1860s. In his view, what was Anthony's primary motivation for her involvement in labor issues? What concerns did she have for the plight of lower-class working women?

5. In his examination of Anthony's 1873 trial for voting illegally, Godfrey D. Lehman discusses a number of legal irregularities that occurred. He maintains that Anthony did not receive a fair trial for political reasons. Do you agree or disagree with Lehman's assertion? Defend your answer, citing the article.

6. Anthony worked to unite different women's groups, as Ellen Carol DuBois relates. According to DuBois, how did many of these organizations differ from Anthony's National Woman Suffrage Association? What concessions and compromises did Anthony have to make in order to find common ground, and what was her objective in doing so?

7. Mildred Adams traces Anthony's travels in England and Europe during 1883. Which of Anthony's overseas experiences does the author cite as convincing her of the need for an international women's organization? What goals did Anthony have for this international movement? What did it actually accomplish?

8. In her article about Anthony's work in promoting coeducation, Zoë Ingalls focuses on the drive to open the University of Rochester to women students. According to Ingalls, what steps did Anthony take to accomplish this goal? What did the success of the coeducation campaign mean to the young women of Rochester, as reported in the article?

9. Describe Anthony's skills as an orator, as listed in Kathleen Barry's essay. How did these skills contribute to Anthony's success as a public reformer, according to Barry? Provide details, quoting from the text.

CHAPTER 3

1. According to Judith E. Harper, on what foundation was the friendship of Anthony and Lucy Stone based? What events led to the dissolution of this friendship? How did their growing personal animosity affect the course of the women's suffrage movement?

2. What conception did the general public have concerning Anthony's attitude toward men, as described by Lynn Sherr? In the author's opinion, how did Anthony's actual feelings toward men differ from this popular view? Do you find Sherr's article convincing? Why or why not?

3. Eleanor Flexner compares and contrasts Anthony's two protégées, Carrie Chapman Catt and Anna Howard Shaw. What similarities did the two women share? What were each woman's strengths and weaknesses as a leader? According to Flexner, why did Anthony ultimately choose Catt rather than Shaw as her successor as the president of the National American Woman Suffrage Association?

4. Sara Hunter Graham contends that the younger members of the women's rights movement reworked Anthony's image into "the patron saint of suffrage" by stressing only certain qualities of her personality and life. According to Graham, when did this process begin? How did Anthony's beatification mirror the transformation of the suffrage movement into a less radical and more respectable cause?

APPENDIX OF DOCUMENTS

DOCUMENT 1: ADVOCATING TEMPERANCE

Susan B. Anthony originally devoted her energies to the temperance movement, which advocated abstinence from alcohol. On March 2, 1849, she delivered her first public address at an assembly of the Daughters of Temperance in Canajoharie, New York.

Welcome Ladies, to this, our Hall of Temperance. You have been invited to meet with us this afternoon and for what purpose have you come hither? Are you here to listen to the advancement of new truths, or to hear old ones eloquently portrayed? Permit me *timely* to advise you, that you are destined to disappointment and tell you as nearly as I can, what were our motives in soliciting our friends to mingle with us this afternoon.

We feel that the cause we have espoused, is a common cause, a cause in which you, with us are deeply interested, and we would that some means were devised, by which our brothers and sons shall no longer be allured from the *right*, by the corrupting influence of the fashionable sippings of wine and brandy, those sure destroyers of mental and moral worth, and by which our Sisters and daughters may no longer be exposed to the vile arts of the gentlemanly appearing gallant but really half inebriated seducer. Our motive is to ask of you, council in the formation, and cooperation in the carrying out, of *plans*, which may produce a radical change in our moral Atmosphere. . . .

We count it no waste of time, to go forth through our streets, thus proclaiming our desire for the advancement of our great cause. You, with us no doubt feel that Intemperance is the blighting mildew of all our social connexions. You would be most happy to speed on the time, when no wife shall watch with trembling heart and tearful eye the slow, but sure descent of her idolized companion, down to the loathsome haunts of drunkenness. You would hasten the day when no mother shall have to mourn over a darling son, as she sees him launch his bark on the circling wave of this mighty whirlpool.

How is this great change to be wrought, who are to urge on this vast work of reform, shall it not be we who are most aggrieved by the foul destroyers inroads. Most certainly.

Ann D. Gordon, ed., *The Selected Papers of Elizabeth Cady Stanton and Susan B. Anthony*, vol. 1, *In the School of Anti-Slavery, 1840 to 1866*. New Brunswick, NJ: Rutgers University Press, 1997.

DOCUMENT 2: CRITICISM FROM THE PRESS

At the time Anthony began her career as a temperance worker, women rarely engaged in social activism and refrained from giving public speeches. Anthony was willing to flout these conventions in order to promote her cause, but she often received unfavorable press for doing so, as in the following newspaper report on a temperance lecture that she delivered in Utica, New York.

We conceived a very unfavorable opinion of this *Miss* Anthony when she performed in this city on a former occasion, but we confess that, after listening attentively to her discourse last evening, we were inexpressibly disgusted with the impudence and impiety evinced in her lecture. Personally repulsive, she seems to be laboring under feelings of strong hatred towards male men, the effect, we presume, of jealousy and neglect. She spent some hour or so to show the evils endured by the mothers, wives and daughters of drunkards. She gravely announced that the evil is a great one, and that no remedy might hopefully be asked from licentious statesmen nor from ministers of the gospel, who are always well fed and clothed and don't care for oppressed women. Prominent among the remedies which she suggested for the evils which she alleges to exist, are complete enfranchisement of women, allowing them the run of the legislative halls, ballot-box, etc. With a degree of impiety which was both startling and disgusting, this shrewish *maiden* counseled the numerous wives and mothers present to separate from their husbands whenever they became intemperate, *and particularly not to allow the said husbands to add another child to the family* (probably no *married* advocate of woman's rights would have made this remark). Think of such advice given in public by one who claims to be a *maiden* lady!

Miss Anthony may be a very respectable lady, but such conversation is certainly not calculated to enhance public regard for her. . . . She announced quite confidently that wives don't de facto love their husbands if they are dissipated. Everyday observation proves the utter falsity of this statement, and if there is one characteristic of the sex which more than another elevates and ennobles it, it is the *persistency* and intensity of woman's love for man. But what does Miss Anthony know of the thousand delights of married life; of the sweet stream of affection, of the golden ray of love which beams ever through life's ills? Bah! Of a like disgusting character was her advice to mothers about not using stimulants, even when prescribed by physicians, for the benefit of the young. What in the name of crying babies does Miss Anthony know about such matters?

In our humble judgment, it is by no means complimentary to wives and mothers to be found present at such discourses, encouraging such untruthful and pernicious advice. If Miss Anthony's ideas were practically applied in the relations of life, women would sink from the social elevation they now hold and become the mere *appendages* of men. Miss Anthony concluded with a flourish of trumpets, that the woman's rights question could not be put down, that women's souls were beginning to expand, etc., after which she gathered her short skirts about her tight pants, sat down and wiped her spectacles.

Utica (N.Y.) Evening Telegraph, April 28, 1853.

DOCUMENT 5: NO MORE BRAINS THAN A WOMAN

A schoolteacher for over a decade, Anthony was an avid attendee of educational conventions. However, her experiences at these meetings mirrored those in the temperance movement, where she often faced social disapproval if she attempted to address the audience concerning the issues under debate. The following passage describes the uproar Anthony caused at the 1853 state teachers' convention in Rochester, New York, when she sought permission to speak.

In 1853, the annual convention being held in Rochester, her place of residence, Miss Anthony conscientiously attended all the sessions through three entire days. After having listened for hours to a discussion as to the reason why the profession of teacher was not as much respected as that of the lawyer, minister, or doctor, without once, as she thought, touching the kernel of the question, she arose to untie for them the Gordian knot, and said, "Mr. President." If all the witches that had been drowned, burned, and hung in the Old World and the New had suddenly appeared on the platform, threatening vengeance for their wrongs, the officers of that convention could not have been thrown into greater consternation.

There stood that Quaker girl, calm and self-possessed, while with hasty consultations, running to and fro, those frightened men could not decide what to do; how to receive this audacious invader of their sphere of action. At length President [Charles] Davies, of West Point, in full dress, buff vest, blue coat, gilt buttons, stepped to the front, and said, in a tremulous, mocking tone, "What will the lady have?" "I wish, sir, to speak to the question under discussion," Miss Anthony replied. The Professor, more perplexed than before, said: "What is the pleasure of the Convention?" A gentleman moved that she should be heard; another seconded the motion; whereupon a discussion pro and con followed, lasting full half an hour, when a vote of the men only was taken, and permission granted by a small majority; and lucky for her, too, was it, that the thousand women crowding that hall could not vote on the question, for they would have given a solid "no." The president then announced the vote, and said: "The lady can speak."

We can easily imagine the embarrassment under which Miss Anthony arose after that half hour of suspense, and the bitter hostility she noted on every side. However, with a clear, distinct voice, which filled the hall, she said: "It seems to me, gentlemen, that none of you quite comprehend the cause of the disrespect of which you complain. Do you not see that so long as society says a woman is incompetent to be a lawyer, minister, or doctor, but has ample ability to be a teacher, that every man of you who chooses this profession tacitly acknowledges that he has no more brains than a woman? And this, too, is the reason that teaching is a less lucrative profession, as here men must compete with the cheap labor of woman. Would you exalt your profession, exalt those who labor with you. Would you make it more lucrative, increase the salaries of the women engaged in the noble work of educating our future Presidents, Senators, and Congressmen."

Elizabeth Cady Stanton, Susan B. Anthony, and Matilda Joslyn Gage, eds., *History of Woman Suffrage*, vol. 1. New York: Fowler and Wells, 1881.

DOCUMENT 4: THE RIGHT TO EVERY DOLLAR SHE EARNS

As a reformer, Anthony spent much of her time on the road, delivering lectures in faraway towns. During her travels, she always kept an eye out for incidents that illustrated the need for improvements in women's legal and political rights. In the following letter to her family, written in January 1856, Anthony depicts the financial plight of the wives of the innkeepers that she met on her journey.

We stopped at a little tavern where the landlady was not yet twenty and had a baby fifteen months old. Her supper dishes were not washed and her baby was crying, but she was equal to the occasion. She rocked the little thing to sleep, washed the dishes and got our supper; beautiful white bread, butter, cheese, pickles, apple and mince pie, and excellent peach preserves. She gave us her warm bedroom to sleep in, and on a row of pegs hung the loveliest embroidered petticoats and baby clothes, all the work of that young woman's fingers, while on a rack was her ironing perfectly done, wrought undersleeves, baby dresses, embroidered underwear, etc. She prepared a 6 o'clock breakfast for us, fried pork, mashed potatoes, mince pie, and for me, at my especial request, a plate of delicious baked sweet apples and a pitcher of rich milk. Now for the moral of this story: When we came to pay our bill, the dolt of a husband took the money and put it in his pocket. He had not lifted a hand to lighten that woman's burdens, but had sat and talked with the men in the bar room, not even caring for the baby, yet the law gives him the right to every dollar she earns, and when she needs two cents to buy a darning needle she has to ask him and explain what she wants it for.

Here where I am writing is a similar case. The baby is very sick with the whooping cough; the wife has dinner to get for all the boarders, and no help; husband standing around with his hands in his pockets. She begs him to hold the baby for just ten minutes, but before the time is up he hands it back to her, saying, "Here, take this child, I'm tired." Yet when we left he was on hand to receive the money and we had to give it to him.

Ida Husted Harper, *The Life and Work of Susan B. Anthony*, vol. 1. Indianapolis: Hollenbeck Press, 1898.

DOCUMENT 5: LEGALIZED ROBBERY

During the late 1850s, Anthony served as the New York agent for the American Anti-Slavery Society, organizing groups of field lecturers on tours across the state. Under the influence of nationally prominent abolitionists, Anthony's own speeches became more passionate and dynamic, as evidenced in the following excerpt from her 1857 address entitled "What Is American Slavery?"

What is American Slavery? It is the Legalized Systematized robbery of the bodies and souls of nearly four millions of men, women and children. It is the Legalized traffic in God's Image; It is the buying and selling of Jesus Christ himself on the auction block, as Merchandise, as chattel property, in the person of the outraged slave; For the Divine Jesus said, "Inasmuch as ye do it unto one of the least of these, my brethren, ye do it unto me."

What is American Slavery? It is the depriving of four millions of native born citizens of these United States, of their inalienable right to life, liberty, and the pursuit of happiness. It is the robbing of every sixth man, woman and child, of this glorious republic, of their God-given right—the ownership and control of their own persons, to the earning of their own hands and brains, to the exercise of their own consciences and wills, to the possession and enjoyment of their own homes. It is the sundering of what God has joined together, the divorcing of husbands and wives, parents and children, brothers and sisters. It is the robbery of every comfort, and every possession, sacred to a child of earth and an heir of Heaven. American Slavery? It is a wholesale system of wrong and outrage perpetrated on the bodies and souls of these millions of God's children. Its the legalized prostitution of nearly two millions of the daughters of this proud republic; it is the blotting out from the soul of womanhood, the divine spark of purity, the god of her inheritance. It is the abomination of desolation spoken of by the prophet Daniel, engrafted into the very heart of the American government, it is all and every villainy . . . consolidated into one. It is theft, robbery, piracy, murder. It is avarice, covetousness, lust, licentiousness, concubinage, polygamy; it is atheism, blasphemy, and sin against the Holy Ghost.

Judith E. Harper, *Susan B. Anthony: A Biographical Companion*. Santa Barbara, CA: ABC-CLIO, 1998.

DOCUMENT 6: RISE UP WITH HONEST PURPOSE

As the women's rights movement ground to a halt during the Civil War, Anthony endeavored to keep the flame alive through the forma-

tion of the Woman's National Loyal League. This organization's main purpose was to work for the abolition of slavery, but by encouraging women to take political action, it also promoted the ideology of the women's movement. The following passage is excerpted from Anthony's speech during a meeting of the league on May 14, 1863.

There is great fear expressed on all sides lest this war shall be made a war for the negro. I am willing that it shall be: I am ready to admit that it is a war for the negro. It is a war to found an empire on the negro in slavery, and shame on us if we make it not a war to establish the negro in freedom! It is a war for the elevation of humanity. . . .

It is the women of the North who are assembled here today—the women who have been wont to consider themselves irresponsible for the conduct of the affairs of the nation. And indeed they have no direct responsibility, for they have been content to accept whatever conditions of politics or morals the ruling class has been pleased to make. . . .

The point I wish to make here is this, that the hour is fully come, when woman shall no longer be the passive recipient of whatever morals and religion the trade and politics of the nation may decree; but that she shall now assume her God-given responsibilities, and make herself what she is clearly designed to be, the educator of the race. Let her no longer be the mere reflector, the echo of the worldly pride and ambition of the other half of the race. . . .

And now, women of the North, I ask you to rise up with earnest, honest purpose, to speak the true word and do the just work, in season and out of season. I ask you to forget that you are women, and go forward in the way of right, fearlessly, as independent human beings, responsible to God alone for the discharge of every duty, for the faithful use of every gift, for the multiplying tenfold every talent the good Father has given you. Forget conventionalisms; forget what the world will say, whether you are in your place or out of your place; think your best thoughts, speak your best words, do your best works, looking only to suffering humanity, your own conscience, and God for approval.

Proceedings of the Meeting of the Loyal Women of the Republic, Held in New York, May 14, 1863. New York, 1863.

DOCUMENT 7: A CALL FOR UNIVERSAL SUFFRAGE

After the end of the Civil War, it became increasingly clear that Congress intended to grant black men the right to vote while excluding women. In response, Anthony and her colleagues in the women's rights movement formed the American Equal Rights Association, which advocated suffrage for all adult citizens regardless of race or sex. Anthony delineated the association's history and goals in her December 6, 1866, speech at the Cooper Institute in New York City.

The American Equal Rights Association was formed last spring for the purpose of demanding of this nation the establishment, at this hour, of a genuine republican form of government. We felt—the little handful of men and women, black and white, who formed the association—that something more was to be done than merely to hope for the recognition of the rights of the citizens from a partial Legislature. . . . There are others who say that this is the hour for the establishment only of the equality of the races, that is, the black race shall be brought on to a level with the white race. We go beyond this; we believe that this is the hour to establish the equality of every individual who is subject to the government of the United States—not the hour for the races, but the hour for human beings to be established in equality. Thus we occupy a position above that of any other organization in the country. . . . This association is for the express purpose of reminding the American nation that women form a part of the people. . . . If men will talk in Congress, and out of Congress of impartial suffrage, universal suffrage, we meant to have them understand that women are to be included in its impartiality and universality.

New York World, December 7, 1866.

DOCUMENT 8: AN APPEAL TO BLACK MEN

In October 1868, Anthony sent the following letter to the Colored Men's State Convention in Utica, New York, asking the convention members to insist on suffrage for black women as well as black men. The letter was read at the convention, but the attendees declined to act upon Anthony's request.

Gentlemen: Permit me in behalf of the colored women of the State of New York to urge upon you to extend your demand for the ballot to your wives and daughters—your mothers and sisters. By the laws of our State the grievances of colored women are a thousand fold greater than those of colored men. While colored men not possessed of the requisite $250 to make them voters are exempted from taxation, all colored *women* worth even $50 are compelled to pay taxes. That is, the colored man to-day is worth $200, and is exempt, he dies to-morrow, and his widow is immediately assessed as tax-payer. Then in all trades and professions, your sisters and daughters have not only the obstacles that are everywhere thrown in your way, but also the prejudices and impediments everywhere thrown in woman's way, in addition. Now, Heaven, and all colored men know that the barriers that hedge *your* pathway on every side are most discouraging; I ask you, then, to remember the women by your side, and secure to them all that you claim for yourselves. Now is the time to establish the government of our state, as well as the nation, on the *one Democratic Republican principle*—the *consent of the whole people*—black women and white, as well as black men must now be brought within the body politic.

"Colored Convention in Utica," *Revolution*, October 22, 1868.

DOCUMENT 9: THE WHOLE LOAF OF JUSTICE

The May 1869 convention of the American Equal Rights Association was fraught with turmoil over the question of whether to oppose passage of the Fifteenth Amendment because it did not enfranchise women. Longtime colleagues and friends clashed bitterly over the issue. Frederick Douglass—a former slave, renowned abolitionist, and early supporter of women's rights—was among those who maintained that the ballot was more crucial to black men than to white women. Anthony took the floor to counter his argument.

The question of precedence has no place on an equal rights platform. The only reason why it ever found a place here was that there were some who insisted that woman must stand back & wait until another class should be enfranchised. In answer to that, my friend Mrs [Elizabeth Cady] Stanton & others of us have said, If you will not give the whole loaf of justice to the entire people, if you are determined to give it, piece by piece, then give it first to women, to the most intelligent & capable portion of the women at least, because in the present state of government it is intelligence, it is morality which is needed. We have never brought the question upon the platform, whether women should be enfranchised first or last. . . .

If Mr [Frederick] Douglass had noticed who clapped him when he said "black men first, & white women afterwards," he would have seen that they were all men. The women did not clap him. The fact is that the men cannot understand us women. They think of us as some of the slaveholders used to think of their slaves, all love & compassion, with no malice in their hearts, but they thought "The negro is a poor lovable creature, kind, docile, unable to take care of himself, & dependent on our compassion to keep them"; & so they consented to do it for the good of the slaves. Men feel the same today. Douglass, [Theodore] Tilton, & [Wendell] Phillips, think that women are perfectly contented to let men earn the money & dole it out to us. We feel with Alexander Hamilton, "Give a man power over my substance, & he has power over my whole being." There is not a woman born, whose bread is earned by another, it does not matter whether that other is husband, brother, father, or friend, not one who consents to eat the bread earned by other hands, but her whole moral being is in the power of that person.

When Mr Douglass tells us today that the case of the black man is so perilous, I tell him that wronged & outraged as they are by this hateful & mean prejudice against color, he would not today exchange his sex & color, wronged as he is, with Elizabeth Cady Stanton.

Mr Douglass. Will you allow me a question?

Miss Anthony. Yes; anything for a fight today.

Mr Douglass. I want to inquire whether granting to woman the right of suffrage will change anything in respect to the nature of our sexes.

Miss Anthony. It will change the nature of one thing very much, & that is the pecuniary position of woman. It will place her in a position in which she can earn her own bread, so that she can go out into the world an equal competitor in the struggle for life; so that she shall not be compelled to take such positions as men choose to accord to her & then take such pay as men choose to give her. . . . What we demand is that woman shall have the ballot, for she will never get her other rights until she demands them with the ballot in her hand. It is not a question of precedence between women & black men. Neither has a claim to precedence upon an Equal Rights platform. But the business of this association is to demand for every man black or white, & for every woman, black or white, that they shall be this instant enfranchised & admitted into the body politic with equal rights & privileges.

Ann D. Gordon, ed., *The Selected Papers of Elizabeth Cady Stanton and Susan B. Anthony*, vol. 2, *Against an Aristocracy of Sex, 1866 to 1873*. New Brunswick, NJ: Rutgers University Press, 2000.

DOCUMENT 10: TAXATION WITHOUT REPRESENTATION

In June 1869, Anthony received a letter from a deputy collector of the Internal Revenue Service notifying her about taxes owed on her newspaper. She decided to pay her taxes under protest, for reasons that she explains in the following letter to the deputy collector.

Dear Sir: I have your polite note informing me that as publisher of the *Revolution* I am indebted to the United States government in the sum of $14.10 for the tax on monthly sales of that journal.

Enclosed you will find the amount—*fourteen dollars ten cents*—but you will please understand that I pay it under protest.

The *Revolution*, you are aware, is a journal, the main object of which is to apply to these degenerate times the great principles on which our ancestors fought the battles of the Revolution, and whereon they intended to base our Republican government, viz., that "Taxation and representation should go together"; and that to inflict taxation upon any class of the people, without at the same time conferring upon them the right of representation, is tyranny.

I am not represented in the United States government, and yet that government taxes me; and it taxes me, too, for publishing a paper the chief purpose of which is to point out and rebuke the glaring and oppressive inconsistency between its professions and its practices.

Under the circumstances, the Federal government ought to be ashamed to exact this tax of me. However, as there is such pressing need of money to supply a treasury which is so sadly depleted by extravagant expenditures and clandestine abstractions by its own officials, I consent to contribute to its necessities this large sum ($14.10), assuring you that when the women get the ballot and become their own representatives, as they surely will and that very soon, they will conduct themselves more generously and equitably toward the men than men now do toward them; for we shall then not only *permit* you to pay taxes, but *compel* you to vote also. I had thought of resisting the payment of this tax on high moral grounds, as an unjustifiable exaction, but learning that the courts do not take cognizance of moral questions, I have decided to send you the sum ($14.10) enclosed.

"Miss Anthony's Tax," *Revolution*, June 17, 1869.

DOCUMENT 11: DEFENDING HER RIGHT TO VOTE

In November 1872, Anthony went to her local polling place and cast a ballot in the national election; she was subsequently arrested for voting illegally. Released on bail, Anthony traveled throughout Monroe and Ontario Counties of New York during the next few months, arguing her case in a speech entitled "Is It a Crime for a United States Citizen to Vote?"

Friends and Fellow-citizens: I stand before you to-night, under indictment for the alleged crime of having voted at the last Presidential election, without having a lawful right to vote. It shall be my work this evening to prove to you that in thus voting, I not only committed no crime, but, instead, simply exercised my *citizen's right*, guaranteed to me and all United States citizens by the National Constitution, beyond the power of any State to deny.

Our democratic-republican government is based on the idea of the natural right of every individual member thereof to a voice and a vote in making and executing the laws. We assert the province of government to be to secure the people in the enjoyment of their unalienable rights. We throw to the winds the old dogma that governments can give rights. Before governments were organized, no one denies that each individual possessed the right to protect his own life, liberty and property. And when 100 or 1,000,000 people enter into a free government, they do not barter away their natural rights; they simply pledge themselves to protect each other in the enjoyment of them, through prescribed judicial and legislative tribunals. They agree to abandon the methods of brute force in the adjustment of their differences, and adopt those of civilization. . . .

The preamble of the federal constitution says:

"We, the people of the United States, in order to form a more perfect union, establish justice, insure *domestic* tranquility, provide for the common defence, promote the general welfare and secure the blessings of liberty to ourselves and our posterity, do ordain and establish this constitution for the United States of America."

It was we, the people, not we, the white male citizens, nor yet we, the male citizens; but we, the whole people, who formed this Union. And we formed it, not to give the blessings of liberty, but to secure them; not to the half of ourselves and the half of our posterity, but to the whole people—women as well as men. And it is downright mockery to talk to women of their enjoyment of the blessings of liberty while they are denied the use of the only means of securing them provided by this democratic-republican government—the ballot. . . .

But, it is urged, the use of the masculine pronouns he, his and him, in all the constitutions and laws, is proof that only men were meant to be included in their provisions. If you insist on this version of the letter of the law, we shall insist that you be consistent, and accept the other horn of the dilemma, which would compel you to exempt women from taxation for the support of the government, and from penalties for the violation of laws. . . .

In all the penalties and burdens of the government, (except the military) women are reckoned as citizens, equally with men. Also, in all the privileges and immunities, save those of the jury box and ballot box, the two fundamental privileges on which rest all the others. The United States government not only taxes, fines, imprisons and hangs women, but it allows them to pre-empt lands, register ships, and take out passport and naturalization papers. . . .

The fourteenth amendment [states] in its first sentence: "All persons born or naturalized in the United States and subject to the jurisdiction thereof, are citizens of the United States and of the state wherein they reside."

And the second settles the equal status of all persons—all citizens:

"No state shall make or enforce any law which shall abridge the privileges or immunities of citizens; nor shall any state deprive any person of life, liberty or property, without due process of law, nor deny to any person within its jurisdiction the equal protection of the laws."

The only question left to be settled, now, is: Are women persons? And I hardly believe any of our opponents will have the hardihood to say they are not. Being persons, then, women are citizens, and no state has a right to make any new law, or to enforce any old law, that shall abridge their privileges or immunities. Hence, every discrimination against women in the constitutions and laws of the several states, is to-day null and void, precisely as is every one against negroes.

An Account of the Proceedings on the Trial of Susan B. Anthony. Rochester, NY: Daily Democrat and Chronicle Book Print, 1874.

DOCUMENT 12: ANTHONY'S STATEMENT AT HER SENTENCING

Anthony's trial was held on June 17, 1873, presided over by Judge Ward Hunt. The judge refused to allow Anthony to testify on her own behalf during the trial, and he circumvented the jury in order to hand down a guilty verdict himself. Before the judge pronounced her sentence, though, he asked Anthony a routine legal question—and she seized the chance to air her argument concerning her case.

Judge Hunt—(Ordering the defendant to stand up), Has the prisoner anything to say why sentence shall not be pronounced?

Miss Anthony—Yes, your honor, I have many things to say; for in your ordered verdict of guilty, you have trampled under foot every vital principle of our government. My natural rights, my civil rights, my political rights, my judicial rights, are all alike ignored. Robbed of the fundamental privilege of citizenship, I am degraded from the status of a citizen to that of a subject; and not only myself individually, but all of my sex, are, by your honor's verdict, doomed to political subjection under this, so-called, form of government.

Judge Hunt—The Court cannot listen to a rehearsal of arguments the prisoner's counsel has already consumed three hours in presenting.

Miss Anthony—May it please your honor, I am not arguing the question, but simply stating the reasons why sentence cannot, in justice, be pronounced against me. Your denial of my citizen's right to vote, is the denial of my right of consent as one of the governed, the denial of my right of representation as one of the taxed, the denial of my right to a trial by a jury of my peers as an offender against law, therefore, the denial of my sacred rights to life, liberty, property and—

Judge Hunt—The Court cannot allow the prisoner to go on.

Miss Anthony—But your honor will not deny me this one and only poor privilege of protest against this high-handed outrage upon my citizen's rights. May it please the Court to remember that since the day of my arrest last November, this is the first time that either myself or any person of my disfranchised class has been allowed a word of defense before judge or jury—

Judge Hunt—The prisoner must sit down—the Court cannot allow it.

Miss Anthony—All of my prosecutors, from the 8th ward corner grocery politician, who entered the complaint, to the United States Marshal, Commissioner, District Attorney, District Judge, your honor on the bench, not one is my peer, but each and all are my political sovereigns; and had your honor submitted any case to the jury, as was clearly your duty, even then I should have had just cause of protest, for not one of those men was my peer; but, native or foreign born, white or black, rich or poor, educated or ignorant, awake or asleep, sober or drunk, each and every man of them was my political superior; hence, in no sense, my peer. Even, under such circumstances, a commoner of England, tried before a jury of Lords, would have far less cause to complain than should I, a woman, tried before a jury of men. Even my counsel, the Hon. Henry R. Selden, who has argued my cause so ably, so earnestly, so unanswerably before your honor, is my political sovereign. Precisely as no disfranchised person is entitled to sit upon a jury, and no woman is entitled to the franchise, so, none but a regularly admitted lawyer is allowed to practice in the courts, and no woman can gain admission to the bar—hence, jury, judge, counsel, must all be of the superior class.

Judge Hunt—The Court must insist—the prisoner has been tried according to the established forms of law.

Miss Anthony—Yes, your honor, but by forms of law all made by men, interpreted by men, administered by men, in favor of men, and against women; and hence, your honor's ordered verdict of guilty, against a United States citizen for the exercise of *"that citizen's right to vote,"* simply because that citizen was a woman and not a man. But, yesterday, the same man made forms of law, declared it a crime punishable with $1,000 fine and six months' imprisonment, for you, or me, or any of us, to give a cup of cold water, a crust of bread, or a night's shelter to a panting fugitive as he was tracking his way to Canada. And every man or woman in whose veins coursed a drop of human sympathy violated that wicked law, reckless of consequences, and was justified in so doing. As then, the slaves who got their freedom must take it over, or under, or through the unjust forms of law, precisely so, now, must women, to get their right to a voice in this government, take it; and I have taken mine, and mean to take it at every possible opportunity.

Judge Hunt—The Court orders the prisoner to sit down. It will not allow another word.

Miss Anthony—When I was brought before your honor for trial, I hoped for a broad and liberal interpretation of the Constitution and its recent amendments, that should declare all United States citizens under its protecting ægis—that should declare equality of rights the national guarantee to all persons born or naturalized in the United States. But failing to get this justice—failing, even, to get a trial by a jury *not* of my peers—I ask not leniency at your hands—but rather the full rigors of the law.

Judge Hunt—The Court must insist—

(Here the prisoner sat down.)

Judge Hunt—The prisoner will stand up.

(Here Miss Anthony arose again.)

The sentence of the Court is that you pay a fine of one hundred dollars and the costs of the prosecution.

Miss Anthony—May it please your honor, I shall never pay a dollar of your unjust penalty. All the stock in trade I possess is a $10,000 debt, incurred by publishing my paper—*The Revolution*—four years ago, the sole object of which was to educate all women to do precisely as I have done, rebel against your man-made, unjust, unconstitutional forms of law, that tax, fine, imprison and hang women, while they deny them the right of representation in the government; and I shall work on with might and main to pay every dollar of that honest debt, but not a penny shall go to this unjust claim. And I shall earnestly and persistently continue to urge all women to the practical recognition of the old revolutionary maxim, that "Resistance to tyranny is obedience to God."

Judge Hunt—Madam, the Court will not order you committed until the fine is paid.

An Account of the Proceedings on the Trial of Susan B. Anthony. Rochester, NY: Daily Democrat and Chronicle Book Print, 1874.

DOCUMENT 13: THE DECLARATION OF RIGHTS FOR WOMEN

The United States celebrated its centennial in 1876 with a large exposition in Philadelphia. Anthony, Elizabeth Cady Stanton, and Matilda Joslyn Gage drafted a Declaration of Rights for Women and asked for permission to read it during the Fourth of July ceremony at Independence Hall. Their request was denied, so Anthony decided to simply disrupt the ceremony. She handed out copies of the declaration to the stunned dignitaries, then left the hall and proceeded to an outdoor platform, where she read the declaration to a large crowd.

While the nation is buoyant with patriotism, and all hearts are attuned to praise, it is with sorrow we come to strike the one discordant note, on this one-hundredth anniversary of our country's birth. When subjects of kings, emperors, and czars, from the old world join in our national jubilee, shall the women of the republic refuse to lay their hands with benedictions on the nation's head? Surveying America's exposition, surpassing in magnificence those of London, Paris, and Vienna, shall we not rejoice at the success of the youngest rival among the nations of the earth? May not our hearts, in unison with all, swell with pride at our great achievements as a people; our free speech, free press, free schools, free church, and the rapid progress we have made in material wealth, trade, commerce and the inventive arts? And we do rejoice in the success, thus far, of our experiment of self-government. Our faith is firm and unwavering in the broad principles of human rights proclaimed in 1776, not only as abstract truths, but as the cornerstones of a republic. Yet we cannot forget, even in this glad hour, that while all men of every race, and clime, and condition, have been invested with the full rights of citizenship under our hospitable flag, all women still suffer the degradation of disfranchisement. . . .

Woman's degraded, helpless position is the weak point in our institutions to-day. . . . It was the boast of the founders of the republic, that the rights for which they contended were the rights of human nature. If these rights are ignored in the case of one-half the people, the nation is surely preparing for its downfall. Governments try themselves. The recognition of a governing and a governed class is incompatible with the first principles of freedom. Woman has not been a heedless spectator of the events of this century, nor a dull listener to the grand arguments for the equal rights of humanity. From the earliest history of our country woman has shown equal devotion with man to the cause of freedom, and has stood firmly by his side in its defense. Together, they have made this country what it is. Woman's wealth, thought and labor have cemented the stones of every monument man has reared to liberty. And now, at the close of a hundred years, as the hour-hand of the great clock that marks the centuries points to 1876, we declare our faith in the principles of self-government; our full equality with man in natural rights; that woman was made first for her own happiness, with the absolute right to herself—to all the opportunities and advantages life affords for her complete development; and we deny that dogma of the centuries, incorporated in the codes of all nations—that woman was made for man—her best interests, in all cases, to be sacrificed to his will. We ask of our rulers, at this hour, no special favors, no special privileges, no special legislation. We ask justice, we ask equality, we ask that all the civil and political rights that belong to citizens of the United States, be guaranteed to us and our daughters forever.

Elizabeth Cady Stanton, Susan B. Anthony, and Matilda Joslyn Gage, eds., *History of Woman Suffrage*, vol. 3. Rochester, NY: Charles Mann, 1886.

DOCUMENT 14: WAGES AND VOTES

Anthony's most successful lecture, entitled "Woman Wants Bread, Not the Ballot," tackled the argument that women needed financial security more than suffrage. In Anthony's opinion, women needed both—and they would have more leverage to improve their economic state if they possessed the political power of the franchise. Anthony delivered many versions of this speech throughout the 1870s; the following text was compiled from a collection of handwritten notes and newspaper reports by Anthony's first biographer, Ida Husted Harper.

My purpose tonight is to demonstrate the great historical fact that disfranchisement is not only political degradation, but also moral, social, educational and industrial degradation; and that it does not matter whether the disfranchised class live under a monarchial or a republican form of government, or whether it be white working-men of England, negroes on our southern plantations, serfs of Russia, Chinamen on our Pacific coast, or native born, tax-paying women of this republic. Wherever, on the face of the globe or on the page of history, you show me a disfranchised class, I will show you a degraded class of labor. Disfranchisement means inability to make, shape or control one's own circumstances. The disfranchised must always do the work, accept the wages, occupy the position the enfranchised assign to them. The disfranchised are in the position of the pauper. You remember the old adage, "Beggars must not be choosers"; they must take what they can get or nothing! That is exactly the position of women in the world of work today; they can not choose. If they could, do you for a moment believe they would take the subordinate places and the inferior pay? Nor is it a "new thing under the sun" for the disfranchised, the inferior classes weighed down with wrongs, to declare they "do not want to vote." The rank and file are not philosophers, they are not educated to think for themselves, but simply to accept, unquestioned, whatever comes. . . .

I believe that by nature men are no more unjust than women. If from the beginning women had maintained the right to rule not only themselves but men also, the latter today doubtless would be occupying the subordinate places with inferior pay in the world of work; women would be holding the higher positions with the big salaries; widowers would be doomed to a "life interest of one-third of the family estate"; husbands would "owe service" to their wives, so that every one of you men would be begging your good wives, "Please he so kind as to 'give me' ten cents for a cigar." The principle of self-government can not be violated with impunity. The individual's right to it is sacred—regardless of class, caste, race, color, sex or any other accident or incident of birth. What we ask is that you shall cease to imagine that women are outside this law, and that you shall come into the knowledge that disfranchisement means the same degradation to your daughters as to your sons.

Ida Husted Harper, *The Life and Work of Susan B. Anthony*, vol. 2. Indianapolis: Bowen-Merrill, 1898.

DOCUMENT 15: A RIDE HOME

In 1883, Anthony made her first voyage to Great Britain and Europe. Her friends intended the trip to be a relaxing vacation for the overworked reformer, but in between her sightseeing, Anthony managed to meet with feminists in several countries. She provided more immediate aid to an impoverished mother in Ireland, as she relates in the following letter.

Saturday I sauntered along the streets of Killarney, passed the market, and saw all sorts of poor humanity coming in with their cattle to sell or to buy. Many rode in two-wheeled carts without seat or spring, drawn by little donkeys, and nearly all the women and girls were bareheaded and barefooted. On the bridge I saw some boys looking down. I looked too and there was a spectacle—a ragged, bareheaded, barefooted woman tossing a wee baby over her shoulders and trying to get her apron switched around to hold it fast on her back. I heard her say to herself, "I'll niver do it," so I said, "Boys, one of you run down there and help her." At that instant she succeeded in getting the baby adjusted, and to my horror took up a bundle from the grass and disclosed a second baby! Then *I* went down. I learned that she had just come from the poorhouse, where she had spent six weeks, and before going further had laid her two three-weeks-old boys on the cold, wet grass, while she washed out their clothes in the stream. The clothing was the merest rags, all scrambled up in a damp bundle. She had heard her old mother was ill in Milltown and had " fretted" about her till she could bear it no longer, so had started to walk ten miles to her. I hailed a boy with a jaunting-car—told her to wait and I would take her home—got my luncheon—fed the boy's horse, bought lunch for boy and woman— and off we went, she sitting on one side of the car with her two babies, wet bundle, two milk bottles and rubber appendages, bare feet and flying hair, and I on the other, with the boy in front. For a long way both babies cried; they were blue as pigeons, and had on nothing but little calico slips, no socks even. She had four children older than these—a husband who went to fairs selling papers and anything he could to support them all—and an aged father and mother who lived with them. She said if God had given her only one child, she could still help earn something to live on, but now He had given her two, she couldn't. When we reached Milltown I followed her home. It was in a long row of one-room things with a door—but no window. Some peat was smouldering under a hole in the roof called a chimney, and the place was thick with smoke. On the floor in one corner was some straw with a blanket on it, which she said was her bed; in another were some boards fastened into bed-shape, with straw packed in, and this belonged to her father and mother. Where the four other children, with the chickens and the pig, found their places to sleep, I couldn't see. I went to the home of another tenant, and there again was one room, and sitting around a pile of smoking-hot potatoes on the cold, wet ground—not a board or even a flag-stone for a floor— were six ragged, dirty children. Not a knife, fork, spoon or platter was to be seen. The man was out working for a farmer, his wife said, and the evidences were that "God" was about to add a No. 7 to her flock. What a dreadful creature their God must be to keep sending hungry mouths while he withholds the bread to fill them!

Ida Husted Harper, *The Life and Work of Susan B. Anthony*, vol. 2. Indianapolis: Bowen-Merrill, 1898.

DOCUMENT 16: THE TWO HISTORIANS

While working on the third volume of the History of Woman Suffrage *in the mid-1880s, Anthony stayed for several months at Stanton's home in Tenafly, New Jersey. Stanton's oldest daughter, Margaret Stanton Lawrence, wrote this charming account of the two elderly coauthors' collaboration.*

In the centre of a large room, 20 by 22, with an immense bay window, hard wood floor and open fire, beside a substantial office desk with innumerable drawers and doors, filled with documents,— there sit our historians, surrounded with manuscripts and letters from Maine to Louisiana . . . in the centre of their desk are two ink stands and two bottles of mucilage, to say nothing of divers pens, pencils, scissors, knives, etc., etc. As these famous women grow intense in working up some glowing sentence, or pasting some thrilling quotation from John Stuart Mill, [Alexander] Dumas or Secretan, I have seen them again and again dip their pens in the mucilage and their brushes in the ink . . . it is as good as a comedy to watch these souls from day to day. They start off pretty well in the morning, fresh and amiable. They write page after page with alacrity, they laugh and talk, poke the fire by turn, and admire the flowers I place on their desk each morning. Everything is harmonious for a season, but after straining their eyes over the most illegible, disorderly manuscripts I ever beheld, suddenly the sky is overspread with dark and threatening clouds, and from the adjoining room I hear a hot dispute about something. The dictionary, the encyclopedia . . . are overhauled, tossed about in an emphatic manner for some date, fact, or some point of law or constitution. Susan is punctilious on dates, mother on philosophy, but each contends as stoutly in the other's domain as if equally strong on all points. Sometimes these disputes run so high that down go the pens, one sails out of one door and one out of the other, walking in opposite directions around the estate, and just as I have made up my mind that this beautiful friendship of forty years has at last terminated, I see them walking down the hill, arm in arm . . . to watch the sun go down in all his glory. When they return they go straight to work where they left off, as if nothing happened.

Margaret Stanton Lawrence, "As a Mother," *New Era*, November 1885.

Document 17: The Import of the Right to Vote

In the following suffrage speech from 1888, Anthony points out that the right to vote confers a sense of self-worth on every man who possesses it—while disfranchised women receive the painful message that they cannot be trusted to exercise the right to vote with sound judgment.

What is this little thing that we are asking for? It seems so little; it is yet everything. . . . What does your right to vote in this country, men and brethren, say to you? What does that right say to every possible man, native and foreign, black and white, rich and poor, educated and ignorant, drunk and sober, to every possible man outside the State prison, the idiot and the lunatic asylums? What does it everywhere under the shadow of the American flag say to every man? It says, "Your judgment is sound, your opinion is worthy to be counted." That is it. And now, on the other hand, what does it say to every possible woman, native and foreign, black and white, rich and poor, educated and ignorant, virtuous and vicious, to every possible woman under the shadow of our flag? It says, "Your judgment is not sound, your opinion is not worthy to be counted." Do you not see how this fact that every possible man's opinion the moment he arrives at the age of twenty one is thus respected, and thus counted, educates all men into the knowledge that they possess the political authority of every other man? The poorest ditch-digger's opinion counts for just as much as does the opinion of the proudest millionaire. It is a good thing; I believe in it. I would not take from the most ignorant man under the shadow of the flag the right to vote, but I do want to make you understand the difference in our position. I want to say to you what all of you know, that if there was still left under the shadow of the flag any class of men who are still disfranchised, that class would rise in rebellion against the government before it would submit to the outrage. We women cannot rise in open rebellion. Men are our fathers and brothers and husbands and sons. But we shall stand and plead and demand the right to be heard, and not only to be heard, but to have our votes counted and coined into law, until the very crack of doom, if need be.

Woman's Journal, June 9, 1888.

DOCUMENT 18: HIS EQUAL, NOT HIS SLAVE

Anthony was frequently portrayed by the press and political enemies as a bitter spinster, but in reality she received a number of marriage proposals during her life—all of which she turned down. In an 1895 interview, she gave her explanation for why she never said yes to any of her suitors.

I have not yet had a man ask me to be his companion. He has asked me to let him love; and he has said his home needed a housekeeper, and that his children—oh! so many widowers have said this—needed some one to guide their growing minds. I have also had men tell me that together we could be very happy, I at home and he at work. But I have never, and shall never, accept such a proposal. When a man says to me, "Let us work together in the great cause you have undertaken, and let me be your companion and aid, for I admire you more than I have ever admired any other woman," then I shall say, "I am yours truly"; but he must ask me to be his equal, not his slave. As for support! I think a woman should be ashamed to have her husband support her.

New York Recorder, February 16, 1895.

DOCUMENT 19: DRESS REFORM

Like many of her peers in the early women's rights movement, Anthony attempted to wear bloomers for a brief period of time during the 1850s, but the ridicule she experienced was too great to bear. She never again attempted to appear in public in anything besides long skirts, but when bloomers and divided skirts became more acceptable in the 1890s, she applauded the trend.

I am glad to see women asserting themselves in this matter. Not so much because I particularly want them to don bloomers rather than any other style of dress, but because all such movements show that woman is declaring her right to be untrammeled, not only in matters of dress, but opinions as well.

Why, pray tell me, hasn't a woman as much right to dress to suit herself as a man? If he wants to dress in or out of style nobody dares to comment upon it. Certainly the condition of woman is much better today than it was, say, half a century or so ago, but she will never be in her rightful position until she has equal suffrage with man.

We haven't far to look for the reason that prevents many women who advocate just the reform in dress that is causing so much talk now from adopting it, for men must be consulted and pleased in all these matters.

Now, when woman is enfranchised, she will dress as she pleases, and she will dress according to the business that she is engaged in. She won't go in a factory with long sleeves and flowing skirts. She will dress according to good, common sense and her occupation.

"Susan B. Anthony Does Not Practice Her Preaching on Dress Reform," *St. Louis Republic,* May 5, 1895.

DOCUMENT 20: AN ABUSE OF AUTHORITY

The following passage is taken from Anthony's article entitled "The Necessity of Woman Suffrage," written during the California state suffrage campaign of 1896. She lists examples of unreasonable restrictions that men place on women, often in the guise of protecting women's safety or morals.

From time immemorial the rule has been not to punish the male offender, but to get the victim out of his way. If a little girl is bullied and abused by a little boy while out in the yard at play the girl is taken into the house while the boy is left in full possession of the yard. If women are insulted on the street at night the authorities, instead of making the streets safe for them, insist that they remain indoors. Some places have gone so far as to make it a finable offense for women to be out after a certain hour. Even in the matter of woman's dress men have arrogated to themselves authority, and whether it was a Mother Hubbard wrapper or a bloomer costume, have taken legislative action prohibiting it. At Huntington, Long Island, the School Board forbade the women teachers to ride to school on bicycles, "as it produced immorality among the pupils," but the men teachers were not interfered with. In many places school boards have forbidden women teachers to ride a bicycle, and a number of ministers . . . have preached against it. These are but the expressions of the old idea that the man has dominion over the woman and that she should be subject to his authority in all things.

Susan B. Anthony, "The Necessity of Woman Suffrage," *San Francisco Examiner,* May 17, 1896.

DOCUMENT 21: A FEELING OF FREEDOM

Even as she aged, Anthony continued to be open-minded regarding innovations in society, especially if she felt they were beneficial to women. The bicycle serves as a case in point: Many older people felt that young women looked undignified when riding a bicycle, but Anthony immediately realized the independence that this simple form of transportation could provide. The following quote also illustrates how Anthony could turn almost any subject back to the issue of women's suffrage.

I think it has done a great deal to emancipate women. I stand and rejoice every time I see a woman ride by on a wheel. It gives her a feeling of freedom, self-reliance and independence. The moment she takes her seat she knows she can't get into harm while she is on her bicycle, and away she goes, the picture of free, untrammeled womanhood. . . .

The bicycle also teaches practical dress reform, gives women fresh air and exercise, and helps to make them equal with men in work and pleasure; and anything that does that has my good word. What is better yet, the bicycle preaches the necessity for woman suffrage. When bicyclists want a bit of special legislation, such as side-paths and laws to protect them, or to compel railroads to check bicycles as baggage, the women are likely to be made to see that their petitions would be more respected by the law-makers if they had votes, and the men that they are losing a source of strength because so many riders of the machine are women. From such small practical lessons a seed is sown that may ripen into the demand for full suffrage, by which alone women can ever make and control their own conditions in society and state.

Lynn Sherr, *Failure Is Impossible: Susan B. Anthony in Her Own Words.* New York: Times Books, 1995.

DOCUMENT 22: GAINS VERSUS LOSSES

Newspaper editors became kinder to Anthony over the years, but some still persisted in emphasizing her unmarried state. One 1900 newspaper editorial recounted Anthony's many accomplishments on the occasion of her eightieth birthday—but then closed by remarking that "there is an element of tragedy in the fact that Miss Anthony has missed wifehood and motherhood, the crowning honor and glory of a woman's life." The Cleveland Leader *replied with the following humorous editorial, which Anthony greatly enjoyed.*

It is undeniable that Miss Anthony has missed wifehood and motherhood, and in summing up a woman's life it is only fair that we should count the things she has missed along with the things she has gained. Miss Anthony has gained the love and reverence of millions of people now living and of millions yet to be, but then she has never known the unspeakable bliss of nursing a family of children through the measles, whooping cough and mumps. She has lived a useful and perfectly unselfish life, but she doesn't know a thing in the world about the supreme happiness that lies in being housekeeper, cook, chambermaid, nurse, seamstress, hostess and half-a-dozen other things every day in the year till nervous prostration puts an end to the complicated business.

She has stood on a thousand platforms and listened to the applause of vast audiences, but she doesn't know the glory and honor there is in picking up a bucket of hot water and climbing a step ladder to wash the doors and windows. All the joy and rapture of housecleaning in the beautiful month of May are as a sealed book to her. She has made the life of womankind broader, deeper and higher than women ever dreamed it could be, but she has no conception of the breadth, depth and height of satisfaction to be found in nursing a baby through "three-months-colic."

She has made the world over but she is ignorant of the abandon of joy a woman feels when she makes over an old dress for the third time and then sees John start off on his summer fishing trip. She has been free and independent always and the women who are happier for her work will see that she never lacks for any good thing, but alas, she has never known the ecstasy of asking John for ten cents to pay street-car fare and she has never experienced the bliss of hearing him growl about the price of her Easter bonnet and groan over the monthly grocery bill. Here the "element of tragedy" looms up very large indeed.

It is said that on Miss Anthony's last birthday anniversary she received 3,000 letters congratulatory of the things she has gained in her eighty years of life. But there are wives and mothers who would cheerfully and heartily write her 300,000 more letters congratulatory of the things she has missed.

Ida Husted Harper, *The Life and Work of Susan B. Anthony*, vol. 3. Indianapolis: Hollenbeck Press, 1908.

DOCUMENT 23: GAZING INTO THE FUTURE

As the nineteenth century drew to a close, Anthony was asked to provide her predictions for the world of the twentieth century, particularly the status of women. By the time she wrote the following piece, Anthony had come to the realization that women would not win the right to vote in her lifetime, but she was still highly optimistic about what the future would bring.

The woman of the Twentieth Century will be the peer of man. In education, in art, in science, in literature; in the home, the church, the state; everywhere she will be his acknowledged equal, though not identical with him. We cannot begin to see the good of this recognition.

It is impossible to foretell the exact conditions that will exist in the home; but we may be sure they will be more in accord with enlightened manhood and womanhood than any now known. The children will be better fed and clothed and schooled when the father, together with the mother, remains at home and takes part in their training.

The transition period from absolute subjection inevitably has many crudities, and many mistakes will be made; but we must have faith to believe that the final working out of the great principles of justice and equality into woman's perfect freedom with man will result in something vastly superior to the present. Man himself will be greatly improved when he finds at his own fireside an equal in the person he calls wife.

And this cannot be until she holds in her hand that right preservative of all other rights—the ballot. So the sooner man takes the adjective "male" from all of his creeds, codes and constitutions, and leaves woman to feel her responsibility equally with himself in making and executing all the laws that govern society, the sooner will he begin to reap the harvest of the seed sown in the woman's rights agitation of the nineteenth century.

The Twentieth Century will see man and woman working together to make the world the better for their having lived. All hail to the Twentieth Century!

Susan B. Anthony, "Woman to Have the Ballot," *Brooklyn Daily Eagle*, December 30, 1900.

DOCUMENT 24: COEDUCATION IN THE UNIVERSITIES

One of Anthony's goals was to open America's colleges to women students. In the following interview from 1902, she discusses an unexpected obstacle: Some universities agreed to allow women to attend but then strictly segregated them from the male students, holding special classes for women alone.

We women have to fight continually for our rights and after we get them we have to watch constantly for fear they will be taken away just as we begin to feel safe and comfortable. When they can't keep the girls out of college they resort to "segregation" and it is plain enough why it is done—the girls stand so much higher than the boys that it reflects anything but credit on the latter. Something has to be done or let the men go on record as unable to keep up with the intellectual pace the women set for them. We don't want the sexes separated in the class room. Half the stimulus is in competition and if the boys and girls have separate recitations and examinations, how are we going to tell which rank higher? They must compete with each other—that is where the test and the fun come in.

Oh, if I could but live another century and see the fruition of all the work for women! There is so much yet to be done—I think of so many things I should like to do and say—but I must leave them for a younger generation. We old fighters have prepared the way and it is easier than it was fifty years ago when I got into the harness. Young blood, fresh with enthusiasm and with all the enlightenment of the new century, must now carry on the contest. . . . People who do not look deeply into the subject often declare that the present status of women is simply the result of the evolution of the human race, the natural outcome of civilization and general progress, but as a matter of fact, woman herself has been one of the biggest factors in the progress of humanity. The struggle which she has made and is still making for her rightful place in the world has done much to educate and enlighten the race as a whole. She has had to fight for every step gained, for every concession made, and it looks now as if she would have to fight even more strenuously to maintain her hold on what she has obtained.

Ida Husted Harper, *The Life and Work of Susan B. Anthony*, vol. 3. Indianapolis: Hollenbeck Press, 1908.

DOCUMENT 25: WORKING WOMEN

In a 1905 interview, Anthony expressed her opinion regarding the increase in women working outside the home, especially those employed in factories.

Do I deplore the fact that so many women are being forced into the stress of industrial life? Certainly not. I hope that a constantly increasing number of women will earn their own living instead of marrying men with whom it is impossible to live. It is true, of course, that the uneducated women of the country are not getting as good wages as they should get or as they will get, but they are vastly better off than the same class fifty years ago.

The cry that women did not work then is absurd—they did the hardest kind of menial labor on farms, and they toiled at the loom. The difference is this—that fifty years ago these women were not paid for their labor, while to-day they are.

To-morrow the factory operatives, shop girls and other workers of this country are going to be much better paid than they are now, and they're going to get that better pay through organization.

When the women workers of the United States realize their power and the strength that lies in union, they will form a huge national woman's organization which will, by its sheer bulk and force, wring from the employers more pay, shorter hours, improved working conditions.

Lynn Sherr, *Failure Is Impossible: Susan B. Anthony in Her Own Words.* New York: Times Books, 1995.

DOCUMENT 26: THE FINAL ROLL CALL

On March 13, 1906, Anthony passed away after a brief battle with pneumonia. Anna Howard Shaw remained by her bedside throughout her final hours and later published this account of Anthony's last words.

During the last forty-eight hours of her life she was unwilling that I should leave her side. So day and night I knelt by her bed, holding her hand and watching the flame of her wonderful spirit grow dim. At times, even then, it blazed up with startling suddenness. On the last afternoon of her life, when she had lain quiet for hours, she suddenly began to utter the names of the women who had worked with her, as if in a final roll-call. Many of them had preceded her into the next world; others were still splendidly active in the work she was laying down. But young or old, living or dead, they all seemed to file past her dying eyes that day in an endless, shadowy review, and as they went by she spoke to each of them.

Not all the names she mentioned were known in suffrage ranks; some of these women lived only in the heart of Susan B. Anthony, and now, for the last time, she was thanking them for what they had done. Here was one who, at a moment of special need, had given her small savings; here was another who had won valuable recruits to the Cause; this one had written a strong editorial; that one had made a stirring speech. In these final hours it seemed that not a single sacrifice or service, however small, had been forgotten by the dying leader. Last of all, she spoke to the women who had been on her board and had stood by her loyally so long—Rachel Foster Avery, Alice Stone Blackwell, Carrie Chapman Catt, Mrs. [Harriet Taylor] Upton, Laura Clay, and others. Then, after lying in silence for a long time with her cheek on my hand, she murmured: "They are still passing before me—face after face, hundreds and hundreds of them, representing all the efforts of fifty years. I know how hard they have worked. I know the sacrifices they have made. But it has all been worth while!" . . .

She raised my hand to her lips and kissed it—her last conscious action. For more than thirty hours after that I knelt by her side, but though she clung to my hand until her own hand grew cold, she did not speak again.

She had told me over and over how much our long friendship and association had meant to her, and the comfort I had given her. But whatever I may have been to her, it was as nothing compared with what she was to me. Kneeling close to her as she passed away, I knew that I would have given her a dozen lives had I had them, and endured a thousand times more hardship than we had borne together, for the inspiration of her companionship and the joy of her affection. They were the greatest blessings I have had in all my life.

Anna Howard Shaw, *The Story of a Pioneer.* New York: Harper and Brothers, 1915.

CHRONOLOGY

1820

Susan Brownell Anthony, the second child of Lucy Read and Daniel Anthony, is born on February 15 in Adams, Massachusetts.

1826

The family moves to Battenville, New York, where Anthony's father becomes a prosperous and influential member of the community.

1835

Anthony begins her teaching career during the summer session of her father's school, taking over the instruction of younger students.

1836

Anthony leaves home during the winter months to teach in Easton, New York.

1837

In November, Anthony enrolls as a student at Deborah Moulson's Female Seminary in Pennsylvania. An economic crisis rocks the nation, severely affecting Daniel Anthony's businesses.

1838

Due to her family's financial constraints, Anthony leaves school and returns home to Battenville.

1839

Anthony's parents are forced to sell their house and move to the neighboring village of Hardscrabble. Anthony takes a teaching job at a boarding school in New Rochelle, New York, to help support her family. During the next few years, she moves frequently, working either as a teacher or a governess.

1845

Anthony moves with her parents to a farm in Rochester, New York.

1846

Anthony accepts a position as the headmistress of female students at the Canajoharie Academy in upstate New York. She boards at the house of her cousin, Margaret Caldwell.

1848

In Canajoharie, Anthony joins the local chapter of the Daughters of Temperance. The first convention on women's rights, primarily organized by Elizabeth Cady Stanton, is held on July 19 and 20 in Seneca Falls, New York. Anthony's parents and sister attend a second convention in Rochester on August 2.

1849

Anthony gives her first public speech in a meeting of the Canajoharie Daughters of Temperance. Shortly thereafter, she submits her resignation to the Canajoharie Academy, but she remains in Canajoharie to nurse her ailing cousin through a difficult pregnancy. Caldwell's death devastates Anthony, who returns home to her parents in Rochester. Here she takes over the management of the family farm, continues working for the temperance cause, and grows interested in the anti-slavery movement.

1850

The First National Woman's Rights Convention is held in Worcester, Massachusetts. Anthony reads a newspaper report of the convention that includes the text of a speech by Lucy Stone, which sparks Anthony's interest in women's rights.

1851

In May, while attending an anti-slavery convention in Syracuse, New York, Anthony meets Stanton for the first time. Later that summer, Anthony attends a meeting on coeducation at Stanton's house, where she is introduced to Stone.

1852

In January, Anthony serves as a delegate at a convention held by the Sons of Temperance; after she is refused permission to speak to the assembly, Anthony and a few other women walk out of the hall in silent protest. To provide an alternative, she founds the Woman's State Temperance Society, enlisting Stanton's aid in organizing the group's first convention. In September, Anthony attends the Third National Woman's

Rights Convention in Syracuse, New York, where she meets most of the prominent leaders of the movement.

1853

After conservative men take over the annual meeting of the Woman's State Temperance Society, Anthony and Stanton resign from the organization. The experience convinces Anthony to dedicate her energies to the women's rights movement. She begins by organizing a large petition campaign throughout the state of New York in support of expanding married women's property rights.

1854

In February, Anthony presents six thousand signatures in favor of married women's property rights to the state legislature. While visiting southern cities as part of a lecture tour on women's rights, she witnesses slavery firsthand, solidifying her commitment to abolitionism. On Christmas Day, she embarks on a rigorous petition drive and lecture campaign throughout New York for married women's property rights.

1855

Anthony interrupts her tour in February to present the state legislature with her accumulated petitions, then resumes her campaign until May. She recuperates from her months of grueling travel in Massachusetts, where she makes the acquaintance of William Lloyd Garrison and other leading members of the American Anti-Slavery Society.

1856

During the winter, Anthony again canvasses New York for married women's property rights. She also accepts a position as the New York general agent for the American Anti-Slavery Society.

1857

Anthony devotes much of her time to anti-slavery work but continues to lecture on women's rights. She is forced to cancel the annual National Woman's Rights Convention when Stanton, Stone, and the other usual speakers find themselves too occupied with domestic responsibilities to attend.

1858–1859

As national tensions build over the issue of slavery, Anthony faces increasingly hostile crowds at her anti-slavery speeches. She organizes the Eighth and Ninth National Woman's Rights Conventions and lectures in support of coeducation.

1860

In March, following intense lobbying by Anthony and Stanton, the New York state legislature finally passes the Married Woman's Property Act.

1861

The Civil War breaks out in April. Overriding Anthony's objections, the other feminist leaders decide to suspend the women's rights movement for the duration of the war.

1862

The New York state legislature repeals key sections of the 1860 Married Woman's Property Act.

1863

Anthony and Stanton establish the Woman's National Loyal League to promote the passage of the Thirteenth Amendment. Anthony spends much of the next two years directing the league's petition drive.

1865

In January, Anthony travels to Kansas for an extended visit with her brother. The South surrenders on April 9, ending the Civil War. In early August, Anthony discovers that the proposed Fourteenth Amendment would introduce the word "male" into the Constitution; she immediately returns to the East to try to revitalize the women's rights movement.

1866

Anthony and Stanton organize the Eleventh National Woman's Rights Convention, the first held since the beginning of the war. The convention resolves itself into the American Equal Rights Association, dedicated to securing universal suffrage regardless of race or sex. Anthony conducts a petition campaign in an attempt to convince Congress to revise the wording of the proposed Fourteenth Amendment.

1867

While stumping Kansas in support of a women's suffrage referendum, Anthony and Stanton meet George Francis Train, who promises to fund the publication of a feminist newspaper.

1868

On January 8, Anthony and Stanton publish the first issue of the *Revolution.* The Fourteenth Amendment is ratified by the states. Anthony persuades Senator Samuel C. Pomeroy and Representative George W. Julian to propose a federal amendment for women's suffrage to Congress. She also forms the

Workingwomen's Association and becomes involved in the National Labor Union.

1869

The Fifteenth Amendment is proposed in Congress with wording that specifically excludes women from the right to vote. In May, torn over the question of whether to support or oppose the Fifteenth Amendment, the American Equal Rights Association splits apart: Anthony and Stanton establish the National Woman Suffrage Association (NWSA), while Stone founds the American Woman Suffrage Association (AWSA). In August, Anthony is accused of strikebreaking and forced to resign from the National Labor Union.

1870

Due to financial constraints, Anthony sells the *Revolution* and assumes responsibility for the paper's $10,000 debt. To raise money, she commences a lecture tour on women's suffrage throughout the Midwest.

1871

Anthony and Stanton travel to California on a suffrage lecture tour; Anthony continues up the coast into Oregon, the Washington Territory, and British Columbia.

1872

On November 5, Anthony casts her ballot in the national elections. She is arrested at her Rochester home on November 28 on the charge of voting unlawfully.

1873

During the spring, Anthony lectures throughout Monroe and Ontario Counties in New York in defense of her constitutional right to vote. She stands trial on June 17 and is found guilty, but she refuses to pay her fine.

1874–1875

Anthony lectures throughout the country on the lyceum circuit to earn money for the *Revolution* debt.

1876

On May 1, Anthony repays the last of the *Revolution* debt. She disrupts the July 4 Centennial celebration at Independence Hall in Philadelphia, presenting the acting U.S. vice president with a Declaration of Rights for Women.

1877

Anthony campaigns throughout Colorado in support of the state's referendum on women's suffrage, which fails to pass.

1878

Anthony frames the text of a new women's suffrage amendment, which is introduced to Congress in January by Senator A.A. Sargent. Often referred to as the Susan B. Anthony amendment, it becomes the Nineteenth Amendment to the Constitution in 1920.

1879–1882

During these years, Anthony alternates between lecturing on women's suffrage and collaborating with Stanton and Matilda Joslyn Gage on the first two volumes of the *History of Woman Suffrage*. She also helps to direct the 1882 campaign in support of Nebraska's state referendum on women's suffrage, which is ultimately defeated.

1883

Anthony travels abroad, where she meets British and European feminists and conceives the idea of establishing an international organization for women's rights.

1884

For several months, Anthony stays at Stanton's home while the two coauthors work on the third volume of the *History of Woman Suffrage*.

1887

Anthony and Stone begin discussing a merger of NWSA and AWSA.

1888

The first meeting of the International Council of Women is held on the fortieth anniversary of the Seneca Falls convention.

1890

On February 18, NWSA and AWSA reunite to form the National American Woman Suffrage Association (NAWSA). During the unsuccessful South Dakota state suffrage campaign, Anthony takes note of the leadership abilities of Carrie Chapman Catt and Anna Howard Shaw.

1892

Anthony is elected president of NAWSA.

1893

Anthony supervises NAWSA's campaign in support of the passage of the Colorado state suffrage referendum, which ends in success.

1894–1896

These years are spent in extensive traveling as Anthony leads suffrage campaigns in several states.

1900

Anthony resigns as the president of NAWSA in February, backing Catt's election as her successor. Shortly after returning from her summer lecture tour, Anthony overworks herself trying to secure the necessary funds to open the University of Rochester to women. She meets the university's September 8 deadline, but she suffers a stroke two days later and spends several months convalescing.

1904

During the summer, Anthony travels to Europe to attend a meeting of the International Council of Women and to help organize the International Woman Suffrage Alliance. After Catt steps down from the NAWSA presidency, Anthony persuades Shaw to take over the office.

1906

In February, Anthony travels to Baltimore for the annual NAWSA convention and then to Washington, D.C., for her eighty-sixth birthday celebration, where she delivers her final public remarks. She dies at her home in Rochester on March 13.

FOR FURTHER RESEARCH

COLLECTIONS OF ORIGINAL DOCUMENTS PERTAINING TO SUSAN B. ANTHONY

Mari Jo Buhle and Paul Buhle, eds., *The Concise History of Woman Suffrage*. Urbana: University of Illinois Press, 1978.

Ellen Carol DuBois, ed., *The Elizabeth Cady Stanton–Susan B. Anthony Reader: Correspondence, Writings, Speeches*. Boston: Northeastern University Press, 1992.

Elizabeth Frost and Kathryn Cullen-DuPont, eds., *Women's Suffrage in America: An Eyewitness History*. New York: Facts On File, 1992.

Ann D. Gordon, ed., *The Selected Papers of Elizabeth Cady Stanton and Susan B. Anthony*. 2 vols. to date. New Brunswick, NJ: Rutgers University Press, 1997– .

Winston E. Langley and Vivian C. Fox, eds., *Women's Rights in the United States: A Documentary History*. Westport, CT: Greenwood Press, 1994.

Judith Papachristou, ed., *Women Together: A History in Documents of the Women's Movement in the United States*. New York: Knopf, 1976.

Lana Rakow and Cheris Kramarae, eds., *The Revolution in Words: Righting Women, 1868–1871*. New York: Routledge, 1990.

Lynn Sherr, *Failure Is Impossible: Susan B. Anthony in Her Own Words*. New York: Times Books, 1995.

Elizabeth Cady Stanton, Susan B. Anthony et al., eds., *History of Woman Suffrage*. 6 vols. 1881–1922. Reprint, Salem, NH: Ayer, 1985.

200 Susan B. Anthony

BIOGRAPHIES AND STUDIES OF SUSAN B. ANTHONY

Katharine Anthony, *Susan B. Anthony: Her Personal History and Her Era.* Garden City, NY: Doubleday, 1954.

Elizabeth Anticaglia, "Susan B. Anthony," in *12 American Women.* Chicago: Nelson-Hall, 1975.

Kathleen Barry, *Susan B. Anthony: A Biography of a Singular Feminist.* New York: New York University Press, 1988.

Beverly Beeton and G. Thomas Edwards, "Susan B. Anthony's Woman Suffrage Crusade in the American West," in *Women in the West.* Ed. Glenda Riley. Manhattan, KS: Sunflower University Press, 1982.

Constance Buel Burnett, "Susan B. Anthony," in *Five for Freedom.* New York: Greenwood Press, 1968.

Rheta Childe Dorr, *Susan B. Anthony: The Woman Who Changed the Mind of a Nation.* New York: Frederick A. Stokes, 1928.

George Sherwood Eddy and Kirby Page, "Freedom from Man's Domination: Susan B. Anthony," in *Makers of Freedom: Biographical Sketches in Social Progress.* New York: George H. Doran, 1926.

G. Thomas Edwards, *Sowing Good Seeds: The Northwest Suffrage Campaigns of Susan B. Anthony.* Portland: Oregon Historical Society Press, 1990.

Ida Husted Harper, *The Life and Work of Susan B. Anthony.* 3 vols. 1898–1908. Reprint, Salem, NH: Ayer, 1983.

Judith E. Harper, *Susan B. Anthony: A Biographical Companion.* Santa Barbara, CA: ABC-CLIO, 1998.

M.A. DeWolfe Howe, "Woman Suffrage and Its Napoleon, Susan B. Anthony," in *Causes and Their Champions.* Boston: Little, Brown, 1926.

Denise Bolger Kovnat, "Dear, Blessed Susan B.," *University of Rochester Review,* Fall 1995.

Andrea S. Libresco, "Suffrage and Social Change: The Organizing Strategies of Elizabeth Cady Stanton and Susan B. Anthony," *Social Education,* September 1995.

Alma Lutz, *Susan B. Anthony: Rebel, Crusader, Humanitarian.* Boston: Beacon Press, 1959.

Peter Lyon, "The Herald Angels of Woman's Rights," *American Heritage,* October 1959.

Allen H. Merriam, "Susan B. Anthony (1820–1906), Suffragist," in *American Orators Before 1900: Critical Studies and Sources.* Ed. Bernard K. Duffy and Halford R. Ryan. New York: Greenwood Press, 1987.

Mary D. Pellauer, *Toward a Tradition of Feminist Theology: The Religious Social Thought of Elizabeth Cady Stanton, Susan B. Anthony, and Anna Howard Shaw.* Brooklyn, NY: Carlson, 1991.

Don C. Seitz, "Susan B. Anthony—Sister of Suffrage," in *Uncommon Americans: Pencil Portraits of Men and Women Who Have Broken the Rules.* Indianapolis: Bobbs-Merrill, 1925.

Henry Thomas and Dana Lee Thomas, "Susan B. Anthony," in *Living Biographies of Famous Women.* Garden City, NY: Blue Ribbon Books, 1942.

Henry Thomas and Dana Lee Thomas, "Susan B. Anthony," in *50 Great Americans: Their Inspiring Lives and Achievements.* Garden City, NY: Doubleday, 1948.

Doris Yoakam Twichell, "Susan B. Anthony," in *A History and Criticism of American Public Address.* vol. III. Ed. Marie Kathryn Hochmuth. New York: Longmans, Green, 1955.

Geoffrey C. Ward and Ken Burns, *Not for Ourselves Alone: The Story of Elizabeth Cady Stanton and Susan B. Anthony.* New York: Alfred A. Knopf, 1999.

GENERAL HISTORIES OF THE WOMEN'S RIGHTS MOVEMENT

Margaret Hope Bacon, *Mothers of Feminism: The Story of Quaker Women in America.* San Francisco: Harper & Row, 1986.

Steven M. Buechler, *Women's Movements in the United States: Woman Suffrage, Equal Rights, and Beyond.* New Brunswick, NJ: Rutgers University Press, 1990.

Olivia Coolidge, *Women's Rights: The Suffrage Movement in America, 1848–1920.* New York: E.P. Dutton, 1966.

Ellen Carol DuBois, *Feminism and Suffrage: The Emergence of an Independent Women's Movement in America, 1848–1869.* Ithaca, NY: Cornell University Press, 1978.

Doris Faber, *Petticoat Politics: How American Women Won the Right to Vote.* New York: Lothrop, Lee & Shepard, 1967.

Janet Zollinger Geile, *Two Paths to Women's Equality: Temperance, Suffrage, and the Origins of Modern Feminism.* New York: Twayne, 1995.

Nancy A. Hewitt, *Women's Activism and Social Change: Rochester, New York, 1822–1872.* Ithaca, NY: Cornell University Press, 1984.

Israel Kugler, *From Ladies to Women: The Organized Struggle for Woman's Rights in the Reconstruction Era.* New York: Greenwood Press, 1987.

Suzanne M. Marilley, *Woman Suffrage and the Origins of Liberal Feminism in the United States, 1820–1920.* Cambridge, MA: Harvard University Press, 1996.

William L. O'Neill, *Everyone Was Brave: A History of Feminism in America.* Chicago: Quadrangle Books, 1971.

Anne Firor Scott and Andrew MacKay Scott, *One Half the People: The Fight for Woman Suffrage.* Philadelphia: J.B. Lippincott, 1975.

Andrew Sinclair, *The Better Half: The Emancipation of the American Woman.* New York: Harper & Row, 1965.

Martha M. Solomon, ed., *A Voice of Their Own: The Woman Suffrage Press, 1840–1910.* Tuscaloosa: University of Alabama Press, 1991.

Sally Roesch Wagner, *A Time of Protest: Suffragists Challenge the Republic, 1870–1887.* Carmichael, CA: Sky Carrier Press, 1988.

Doris Weatherford, *A History of the American Suffragist Movement.* Santa Barbara, CA: ABC-CLIO, 1998.

INDEX